More Than 100 Delicious Recipes for Grain-Free, Dairy-Free Desserts

The
PALEO DESSERT BIBLE

ANNA CONRAD

Photography by

J. STANFIELD PHOTOGRAPHY

Skyhorse Publishing

Skyhorse Publishing books may be purchased in bulk at special discounts for sales promotion,
corporate gifts, fund-raising, or educational purposes. Special editions can also be created to
specifications. For details, contact the Special Sales Department, Skyhorse Publishing, 307 West
36th Street, 11th Floor, New York, NY 10018 or info@skyhorsepublishing.com.

Skyhorse® and Skyhorse Publishing® are registered trademarks of Skyhorse Publishing, Inc.®,
a Delaware corporation.

Visit our website at www.skyhorsepublishing.com.

10 9 8 7 6 5 4 3 2

Library of Congress Cataloging-in-Publication Data is available on file.
ISBN: 978-1-62873-621-2

Printed in China

Note

This book is intended as a reference volume only, not as a medical manual. The information given here
is designed to help you make informed decisions about your health. It is not intended as a substitute
for any treatment that may have been prescribed by your doctor. If you suspect that you may have
medical problems, we urge you to seek competent medical help.

{ Contents }

Recipe List   vi

Welcome   xi

Preface   xii

Stocking Your Pantry   xiii

Conversions and Equivalencies   223

Index   226

{ Recipe List }

Drop, Shaped, and Rolled Cookies   1

1. Almond Raisin Cookies   3
2. Almond Prune Cookies   4
3. Ginger Almond Cookies   7
4. Orange Almond Cookies   8
5. Nutty Almond Cookies   11
6. Chocolate Almond Cookies with Dried Cranberries   12
7. Sugar Cookies   15
8. Gingered Sugar Cookies   16
9. Lime Sugar Cookies   19
10. Lemon Sugar Cookies   20
11. Molasses-Spice Cookies   23
12. Molasses-Spice Cookies with Dark Rum Glaze   24
13. Molasses-Spice Cookies with Orange Essence   27
14. Lebkuchen   28
15. Jam Thumbprints   30
16. Almond Blossom Cookies   32
17. Chewy Chocolate Cookies   35
18. Chocolate Chip Cookies   36
19. Almond Butter Cookies   39

Icebox and Cookie Cutter Cookies   41

20. Vanilla Icebox Cookies   43
21. Chocolate Icebox Cookies   44
22. Pine Nut-Raisin Icebox Cookies   47
23. Pecan Sandies   48
24. Thick and Chewy Gingerbread Cookies   51
25. Holiday Cookies   52
26. Jam Sandwiches   55

Brownies and Bar Cookies

Brownies and Bar Cookies   57

27. Lunch Box Brownies   59
28. Fudgy Brownies   60
29. Whoopie Pies   62
30. Vanilla Pudding Bars   64
31. Pecan Bars   66
32. Raspberry Streusel Bars   68
33. Lemon Squares   7
34. Key Lime Bars   7
35. Blondies   75
36. Almond Fudge Bars   76
37. Peach Squares   78
38. Apricot Squares   80
39. Strawberry Squares   82
40. Fig Bars   84
41. Paleo Marshmallows   87

Snack Cakes, Sheet Cakes, Bundt Cakes, and Cupcakes   89

42. Applesauce Snack Cake   90
43. Gingerbread Cake   92
44. Gingerbread Cake with Dried Fruit   94
45. Prune-Nut Bread   97
46. Lazy Daisy Cake   98
47. Almond Meal Cake with Broiled Icing   100
48. Italian Almond Cake   103
49. Individual Bananas Foster Cakes   104
50. Chocolate Cupcakes   107
51. Crème Brûlée   108
52. Chocolate Sheet Cake   110
53. Glazed Chocolate Bundt Cake   112
54. German Chocolate Cake   114
55. Warm Chocolate Fudge Cakes   11

56. Pineapple Cake 118
57. Lemon Pound Cake 121
58. Carrot Cake 122

Pies 125

59. Chocolate Cream Pie 126
60. Key Lime Pie 129
61. Almond Butter Pie 130

Tarts 133

62. Classic Tart Dough 135
63. Strawberry Tart 136
64. Poached Apple and Almond Tart 138
65. Poached Pear and Almond Tart 140
66. Baked Raspberry Tart 144
67. Cranberry Pecan Tart 146
68. Linzertorte 149
69. Lemon Tart 152
70. Chocolate Truffle Tart 155
71. Chocolate Walnut Tart 156
72. Espresso Truffle Tart 160

Fruit Desserts 163

73. Apple Crisp 165
74. Strawberry Shortcakes 166
75. Fresh Blueberry Crumble 168
76. Fresh Peach Crisp 170
77. Fresh Blueberry Cobbler with Soft Cookie Topping 172
78. Skillet Apple Brown Betty 175
79. Summer Berry Gratin 176
80. Summer Berry Bake 179
81. Berry Dessert Pancake 180

82. Blueberry Buckle 182
83. Individual Blackberry-Walnut Buckles 185
84. Cider-Baked Apples with Dried Cranberries 186

Milkshakes, Puddings, and Mousses 189

85. Chocolate Milkshake 19
86. Mocha Frappe 192
87. Chocolate Mousse 195
88. Chilled Lemon Mousse with Raspberry Sauce 196
89. Chocolate Pudding 199
90. Chocolate Banana Pudding 200
91. Vanilla Pudding 203
92. Strawberry Vanilla Pudding 204
93. Peach Vanilla Pudding 207
94. Bread Pudding 208
95. Rich and Creamy Banana Pudding 21

Frostings and Jams 213

96. Chocolate Frosting 215
97. Chocolate Frosting with Orange Essence 216
98. Coconut Frosting 218
99. Pecan Coconut Frosting 219
100. Fruit Jam 22

{ Welcome }

Welcome to *The Paleo Dessert Bible*. I wrote, tested, and edited the recipes in this book in my kitchen located in Chattanooga, Tennessee. My mission with *The Paleo Dessert Bible* was to create a comprehensive collection of my favorite dessert recipes and reformulate them to comply as closely as possible with the paleo diet. I abandoned many of the basic tenets that apply to baking with grains and learned how nut flours, palm sugar, coconut milk, and oil behave when formulating desserts. In many, many instances, the recipes are better when converted to paleo versions. I hope you enjoy these desserts, many of which you will recognize by the titles as classic, all-time favorites. And hopefully, you will consider them to be even better than you remembered.

{ Preface }

The paleo diet does not lend itself to the easy incorporation of dessert recipes into the everyday menu. However, I believe that the paleo diet approach to health could be very important to the health of many people. For that reason, we should find ways to make it accessible, which means indulging in the occasional dessert. With some careful planning, a few desserts on an infrequent basis shouldn't do harm. For the most part, the recipes in this book closely adhere to the paleo diet principles. Yes, you will see normally excluded foods (chocolate, coffee, honey, molasses, maple syrup, palm sugar, tapioca flour, alcohol, etc.) in some of the recipes, because it would be impossible to make desserts without them. But indulging in these desserts on an infrequent basis should not set your health goals too far afield. Just make sure you use high-quality, organic, whole foods and additive-free ingredients whenever possible. For a complete list of foods allowed on the paleo diet, see my first cookbook, *The Paleo Cookbook*.

{ Stocking Your Pantry }

The following is a list of standard ingredients you will need to have in your pantry (in addition to typical baking ingredients) before making the recipes in this book. I've listed suppliers for almond flour as well, because almond flour is the main ingredient in many of the recipes, and the suppliers I list here are the best brands to use, based on my experience. I did not list suppliers for other ingredients because I found that the ingredients are widely available from multiple suppliers without much variation in quality.

ALMOND FLOUR AND ALMOND MEAL: Almond flour and almond meal are made by grinding sweet almonds. Almond flour is finely ground blanched almonds (blanching almonds removes the skin). Almond meal is made with or without the skin on the almonds, and it isn't as finely ground as almond flour. The consistency of almond meal is similar to that of corn meal. I have used almond flour from three different suppliers and found them all to be acceptable in dessert recipes. The almond flour suppliers I used are JK Gourmet (www.jkgourmet.com), Benefit Your Life (www.benefityourlifestore.com), and Honeyville (www.honeyvillegrain.com). I grind my own almond meal from whole almonds, since I use it in smaller quantities.

COCONUT FLOUR: Coconut flour is the meat of a coconut, ground finely and defatted. When purchasing, make sure the ingredients state pure coconut flour, without any added ingredients such as rice flour, sugars, or preservatives. Choose coconut flours that are not pristine white in color, because that may indicate unnecessary processing. The color should be similar to coconut flesh, a little off-white and cream-colored.

COCONUT OIL: Coconut oil is extracted from the coconut flesh (meat). Coconut oil is used in many paleo recipes and is the primary fat used in this cookbook. Choose virgin coconut oil (VCO) that is made from fresh coconut and mechanically pressed to extract the oil. Other forms of coconut oil may be extracted via chemical or high-temperature methods, which can reduce the nutrient content and flavor properties of the oil.

COCONUT MILK: Coconut milk is the liquid that comes from squeezing the meat of fresh coconut. Coconut milk can be thick or thin depending on the fat content, or whether or not a thickener has been added. Canned coconut milk is often diluted with water to achieve a lower fat content. Light coconut milk is the lowest fat-containing coconut milk. The recipes in this book are made with canned coconut milk with a 20 to 22 percent fat content (not light). If possible, choose coconut milk that contains no additional ingredients, other than water. Thickeners such as guar gum are often added and should be avoided if at all possible.

PALM SUGAR: Palm sugar is a nutrient-rich, unrefined, low-glycemic, natural sweetener that is obtained by making several slits in the stem of a palm tree, draining the liquid, and then boiling it until thickened. The boiled product is cooled into cakes and later ground and packaged for sale. Palm sugar is a rich brown color, and some say its taste is superior to that of white granulated sugar. Palm sugar behaves much the same as white granulated sugar in baking applications. Palm sugar is not the same as coconut sugar, which is obtained from the cut flowers of the coconut palm tree. The recipes in this book use palm sugar.

BAKING SODA: Baking soda (sodium bicarbonate) is used in baking as a leavening agent when acidic ingredients are present. Acidic ingredients include phosphates, cream of tartar, lemon juice, yogurt, buttermilk, cacao powder, vinegar, etc. Baking soda reacts with the acidic ingredient and releases carbon dioxide, causing the baked good to rise. Baking soda is often used in combination with baking powder.

BAKING POWDER: Baking powder is a leavening agent composed of a weak acid and a weak base that allows baked goods to rise via an acid-base reaction. Baking powder is used in traditional wheat-based breads where a fermentation reaction (via yeast) is undesirable because of the taste fermentation imparts. Baked goods or breads that use baking powder to create "lift" in the baked good are often called quick breads because of the quick release of carbon dioxide in the acid-base reaction, yielding shorter processing times (no waiting for the bread to rise before baking). Paleo breads, which use nut flours instead of wheat based flours, rise via the same chemical mechanism when using baking powder.

EGGS: Eggs play a critical role in baking by providing protein, fat, and moisture. Protein acts as a binding agent to keep the baked good in one piece, rather than crumbling. Fat and moisture provides an excellent mouth-feel and makes the baked good consumable and pleasant to eat, versus dry and hard to chew or swallow. The recipes in this book use more eggs than most non-paleo recipes might, especially when coconut flour is incorporated, because nut flours tend to absorb more moisture than a traditional grain-based flour. Use eggs from free-range chickens or other game birds when possible. The nutrient profile for free-range birds is more paleo-friendly than those purchased from mass-production farming facilities.

TAPIOCA FLOUR AND ARROWROOT FLOUR: Tapioca flour is derived from cassava root and can be used to make breads as the primary flour component, and as a thickening agent to replace cornstarch or other grain-based thickeners. Arrowroot flour is often used interchangeably with tapioca flour as a thickener and is acceptable for the paleo diet. I used tapioca flour in the recipes in this book in an attempt to minimize the number of ingredients in my pantry. I also found tapioca flour to be a little less expensive than arrowroot flour. Do not confuse tapioca pearls with tapioca flour for the purpose of the recipes in this book. Purchase tapioca in flour form, and be sure to check the ingredients to make sure it isn't adulterated with wheat flour.

HONEY: Honey is a sweetener created by bees, which derive the thick fluid by eating flower nectar and processing it until it dehydrates the sugar and creates natural monosaccharide, fructose, and glucose, with a flavor similar in sweetness to granulated white sugar. Because honey has a low water content, most harmful microorganisms will not grow in it. However, honey may contain dormant endospores that are harmful to the immature intestinal tract of infants, which can cause serious illness or even death. For that reason, honey should not be included in recipes that will be eaten by infants. When possible, purchase raw, locally produced honey, for both environmental reasons and because locally harvested honey will have the flavor of local nectar. Raw honey has a significantly lower glycemic index and higher nutrient content than commercially produced and packaged honey. If you cannot tolerate raw honey or if you will be feeding the baked good to an infant, consider real maple sugar or molasses as a substitute, although the flavor profile will vary when using different sugars. Maple syrup is milder and molasses has a more robust flavor.

MAPLE SYRUP: Maple syrup is a concentrated syrup obtained from the maple tree. In colder climates, the maple tree stores starch in its trunk and roots before wintertime.

The starch is converted to sugar and rises into the sap in the spring. To obtain maple syrup, manufacturers and local artisans bore holes in the tree trunks of maple trees (sugar maple, red maple, and black maple) and boil it down to concentrate. Maple syrup has a glycemic index of approximately 54, and it contains manganese, iron, and calcium. Purchase locally produced maple syrup when possible.

MOLASSES: Molasses is a by-product of the manufacture of granulated sugar, or cane sugar. The syrup's flavor, thickness, and nutritional content vary depending upon whether it's the product of the second or third boiling steps during manufacturing. The first boiling product in sugar manufacture is "cane syrup," not molasses. The second boiling is called second molasses, which has a slightly bitter flavor. The third boiling produces blackstrap molasses, which is famous for it's robust flavor. Blackstrap molasses contains calcium, magnesium, potassium, and iron. One tablespoon of blackstrap molasses is reputed to contain 20 percent of the daily nutritional value for each of these nutrients. Blackstrap molasses is used in many of the recipes in this book.

DARK CHOCOLATE (SOLID AND POWDER): Dark chocolate is used in many of the recipes in this book. Choose the darkest organic form available to you. Try to find chocolate that contains 60 percent or greater cacao. Seventy percent or greater cacao content is ideal. If you find the flavor is too bitter, or you aren't getting the melting properties you need, use a slightly lower cacao content or just give yourself time to adjust to the different flavor profile.

VANILLA EXTRACT: Vanilla extract contains the flavor compound vanillin and is a primary flavor ingredient. Percolating vanilla beans in a solution of ethanol and water creates pure vanilla extract. Purchase "pure" vanilla extract (containing a minimum of 35 percent alcohol and 13.5 ounces per gallon of vanilla beans) for the recipes in this book. Double- and triple-strength vanilla extract may be available in your area. If you use double- or triple-strength pure vanilla extract, you will need to use only a small fraction of the amount of vanilla listed in the recipes in this book. Do not use imitation vanilla extract, as it isn't considered paleo-friendly and is made from wood pulp by-products.

The

PALEO DESSERT BIBLE

ANNA CONRAD

{ Drop, Shaped, and Rolled Cookies }

Almond Raisin Cookies   3

Almond Prune Cookies   4

Ginger Almond Cookies   7

Orange Almond Cookies   8

Nutty Almond Cookies   11

Chocolate Almond Cookies with Dried
    Cranberries   12

Sugar Cookies   15

Gingered Sugar Cookies   16

Lime Sugar Cookies   19

Lemon Sugar Cookies   20

Molasses-Spice Cookies   23

Molasses-Spice Cookies with
    Dark Rum Glaze   24

Molasses-Spice Cookies with
    Orange Essence   27

Lebkuchen   28

Jam Thumbprints   30

Almond Blossom Cookies   32

Chewy Chocolate Cookies   35

Chocolate Chip Cookies   36

Almond Butter Cookies   39

Almond Raisin Cookies

Ingredients

1¼ cups almond flour
½ teaspoon baking powder
½ teaspoon salt
¼ teaspoon ground nutmeg
1 cup coconut oil, softened
2 cups palm sugar
2 large eggs
3 cups almond meal
1½ cups raisins

Preparation

1. Adjust the oven racks to the upper-middle and lower-middle positions, and heat the oven to 325°F. Line two large baking sheets with parchment paper. Whisk flour, baking powder, salt, and nutmeg together in a large bowl.
2. In a separate large bowl, beat the coconut oil and palm sugar together with an electric mixer on medium speed for about 30 seconds or until well combined. Beat in the eggs one at a time until combined (about 30 seconds), scraping down the bowl and beaters as necessary.
3. Reduce the mixer speed to low and slowly add the flour mixture, beating until combined (about 30 seconds). Mix in the almond meal and raisins until just incorporated.
4. Working with about three tablespoons at a time, roll the dough into balls and lay them on the prepared baking sheets, spaced about two inches apart. Flatten cookies to a three-quarter-inch thickness using your palm.
5. Bake the cookies until the edges are set and beginning to brown, but the centers are still soft and puffy (22 to 25 minutes) switching and rotating the baking sheets halfway through baking.
6. Let the cookies cool on the baking sheets for 10 minutes. Serve warm or transfer to a wire rack and cool completely.

Almond Prune Cookies

MAKES 24 COOKIES

Ingredients

1¼ cups almond flour

½ teaspoon baking powder

½ teaspoon salt

¼ teaspoon ground nutmeg

1 cup coconut oil, softened

2 cups palm sugar

2 large eggs

3 cups almond meal

1½ cups prunes

Preparation

1. Adjust the oven racks to the upper-middle and lower-middle positions and heat the oven to 325°F. Line two large baking sheets with parchment paper. Whisk flour, baking powder, salt, and nutmeg together in a large bowl.

2. In a large bowl, beat the coconut oil and palm sugar together with an electric mixer on medium speed for about 30 seconds or until well combined. Beat in the eggs one at a time until combined (about 30 seconds), scraping down the bowl and beaters as necessary.

3. Reduce the mixer speed to low and slowly add the flour mixture, beating until combined (about 30 seconds). Mix in the almonds and prunes until just incorporated.

4. Working with about three tablespoons at a time, roll the dough into balls and lay them on the prepared baking sheets, spaced about two inches apart. Flatten cookies to a three-quarter-inch thickness using your palm.

5. Bake the cookies until the edges are set and beginning to brown, but the centers are still soft and puffy (22 to 25 minutes) switching and rotating the baking sheets halfway through baking.

6. Let the cookies cool on the baking sheets for 10 minutes. Serve warm or transfer to a wire rack and cool completely.

Ginger-Almond Cookies

MAKES 24 COOKIES

Ingredients

1¼ cups almond flour

½ teaspoon baking powder

½ teaspoon salt

¾ teaspoon ground ginger

¼ teaspoon ground nutmeg

1 cup coconut oil, softened

2 cups palm sugar

2 large eggs

3 cups almond meal

Preparation

1. Adjust the oven racks to the upper-middle and lower-middle positions and heat the oven to 325°F. Line two large baking sheets with parchment paper. Whisk flour, baking powder, salt, and ginger together in a large bowl.

2. In a separate large bowl, beat the coconut oil and palm sugar together with an electric mixer on medium speed for about 30 seconds or until well combined. Beat in the eggs one at a time until combined (about 30 seconds), scraping down the bowl and beaters as necessary.

3. Reduce the mixer speed to low and slowly add the flour mixture, beating until combined (about 30 seconds). Mix in the almond meal until just incorporated.

4. Working with about three tablespoons at a time, roll the dough into balls and lay them on the prepared baking sheets, spaced about two inches apart. Flatten cookies to a three-quarter-inch thickness using your palm.

5. Bake the cookies until the edges are set and beginning to brown, but the centers are still soft and puffy (22 to 25 minutes), switching and rotating the baking sheets halfway through baking.

6. Let the cookies cool on the baking sheets for 10 minutes. Serve warm or transfer to a wire rack and cool completely.

Orange Almond Cookies

Ingredients

1¼ cups almond flour
½ teaspoon baking powder
½ teaspoon salt
¾ teaspoon ground ginger
¼ teaspoon ground nutmeg
1 cup coconut oil, softened
2 cups palm sugar
2 large eggs
3 cups almond meal
2 tablespoons orange zest, fresh and grated
1 cup toasted almonds, chopped

Preparation

1. Adjust the oven racks to the upper-middle and lower-middle positions and heat the oven to 325°F. Line two large baking sheets with parchment paper. Whisk flour, baking powder, salt, and ginger together in a large bowl.
2. In a separate large bowl, beat the coconut oil and palm sugar together with an electric mixer on medium speed for about 30 seconds or until well combined. Beat in the eggs one at a time until combined (about 30 seconds), scraping down the bowl and beaters as necessary.
3. Reduce the mixer speed to low and slowly add the flour mixture, beating until combined (about 30 seconds). Mix in the almond meal, orange zest, and almonds until just incorporated.
4. Working with about three tablespoons at a time, roll the dough into balls and lay them on the prepared baking sheets, spaced about two inches apart. Flatten cookies to a three-quarter-inch thickness using your palm.
5. Bake the cookies until the edges are set and beginning to brown, but the centers are still soft and puffy (22 to 25 minutes), switching and rotating the baking sheets halfway through baking.
6. Let the cookies cool on the baking sheets for 10 minutes. Serve warm or transfer to a wire rack and cool completely.

Nutty Almond Cookies

Ingredients

1⅓ cups almond flour
½ teaspoon baking powder
½ teaspoon salt
¾ teaspoon ground ginger
1 cup coconut oil, softened
2 cups palm sugar
2 large eggs
3 cups almond meal
1 cup walnuts, chopped
¼ cup toasted almonds, ground

Preparation

1. Adjust the oven racks to the upper-middle and lower-middle positions and heat the oven to 325°F. Line two large baking sheets with parchment paper. Whisk flour, baking powder, salt, and ginger together in a large bowl.

2. In a separate large bowl, beat the coconut oil and palm sugar together with an electric mixer on medium speed for about 30 seconds or until well combined. Beat in the eggs one at a time until combined (about 30 seconds), scraping down the bowl and beaters as necessary.

3. Reduce the mixer speed to low and slowly add the flour mixture, beating until combined (about 30 seconds). Mix in the almond meal, ground toasted almonds, and chopped walnuts until just incorporated.

4. Working with about three tablespoons at a time, roll the dough into balls and lay them on the prepared baking sheets, spaced about two inches apart. Flatten cookies to a three-quarter-inch thickness using your palm.

5. Bake the cookies until the edges are set and beginning to brown, but the centers are still soft and puffy (22 to 25 minutes), switching and rotating the baking sheets halfway through baking.

6. Let the cookies cool on the baking sheets for 10 minutes. Serve warm or transfer to a wire rack and cool completely.

Chocolate Almond Meal Cookies With Dried Cranberries

MAKES 16 LARGE COOKIES

Ingredients

1¼ cups almond flour

¾ teaspoon baking powder

½ teaspoon baking soda

½ teaspoon salt

1¼ cups almond meal

1 cup pecans, toasted and chopped

1 cup dried cranberries, coarsely chopped

4 ounces non-dairy bittersweet cacao nibs, finely chopped

12 tablespoons coconut oil, softened

1½ cups palm sugar

1 large egg

1 teaspoon vanilla extract

Preparation

1. Adjust the oven racks to the upper-middle and lower-middle positions and heat the oven to 350°F. Line two large baking sheets with parchment paper. Whisk the flour, baking powder, baking soda, and salt together in a medium bowl. In a small bowl, stir almond meal, pecans, cranberries, and cacao nibs together.

2. In a separate large bowl, beat the coconut oil and palm sugar together with an electric mixer on medium speed for about 30 seconds or until well combined. Beat in the egg and vanilla until incorporated (about 30 seconds), scraping down the bowl and beaters as needed.

3. Reduce the mixer speed to low and slowly add the flour mixture, beating until combined (about 30 seconds). Gradually add in the almond meal-cacao nibs mixture until incorporated.

4. Working with ¼ cup at a time, roll the dough into balls and lay them on the prepared baking sheets, spaced about two and a half inches apart. Flatten cookies to a one-inch thickness with your palm.

5. Bake the cookies until the edges are set and beginning to brown, but the centers are still soft and puffy (20 to 25 minutes), switching and rotating the baking sheets halfway through baking. (The cookies will look raw between the cracks and seem underdone.)

6. Let the cookies cool on the baking sheets for 10 minutes. Serve warm or transfer to a wire rack and cool completely.

Making Dough Ahead

The bowl of cookie dough can be wrapped tightly with plastic wrap and refrigerated for up to two days. When ready to use, allow the dough to come to room temperature, then portion and bake as directed. The dough can also be shaped into balls and frozen on a cookie sheet. When they are frozen solid, transfer them to a large freezer bag. To bake, arrange the frozen cookies (do not thaw) on two large parchment-lined baking sheets and bake as directed, increasing the baking time to 25 to 30 minutes.

Sugar Cookies

MAKES 24 COOKIES

Ingredients

2 cups palm sugar

2½ cups almond flour

½ teaspoon baking powder

½ teaspoon salt

14 tablespoons coconut oil, softened

2 teaspoons vanilla extract

2 large eggs

Preparation

1. Adjust an oven rack to the middle position and heat the oven to 350°F. Line two large baking sheets with parchment paper. Spread ½ cup of the palm sugar in a shallow dish for rolling. In a medium bowl, whisk the flour, baking powder, and salt together.

2. In a separate large bowl, beat the coconut oil and remaining 1½ cups palm sugar together with an electric mixer on medium speed for about 30 seconds or until well combined. Beat in the vanilla and then the eggs one at a time until combined (about 30 seconds), scraping down the bowl and beaters as needed.

3. Reduce the mixer speed to low and slowly add the flour mixture, beating until combined (about 30 seconds). Give the dough a few final stirs with a rubber spatula to make sure it is well combined.

4. Working with two tablespoons at a time, roll the dough into balls with wet hands, then coat with the palm sugar. Place balls on the prepared baking sheets, spaced about two inches apart. Flatten the cookies to a three-quarter-inch thickness with the greased bottom of a drinking glass. Sprinkle the remaining palm sugar over the flat tops.

5. Bake the cookies, one sheet at a time, until the edges are set and beginning to brown, but the centers are still soft and puffy (10 to 12 minutes), rotating each baking sheet halfway through the baking. Cookies will spread out and flatten.

6. Let the cookies cool on the baking sheet for 10 minutes. Serve warm or transfer to a wire rack and cool completely.

Gingered Sugar Cookies

Ingredients

2 cups palm sugar

2½ cups almond flour

1 teaspoon grated fresh ginger, or ¼
teaspoon ginger powder

½ teaspoon baking powder

½ teaspoon salt

14 tablespoons coconut oil, softened

2 teaspoons vanilla extract

2 large eggs

Preparation

1. Adjust an oven rack to the middle position and heat the oven to 350°F. Line two large baking sheets with parchment paper. Process ½ cup palm sugar with one teaspoon grated ginger (or ¼ teaspoon ginger powder) in a food processor until fragrant (about 10 seconds). Spread the palm sugar and ginger mixture in a shallow dish for rolling. In a medium bowl, whisk the flour, baking powder, and salt together.

2. In a separate large bowl, beat the coconut oil and remaining 1½ cups palm sugar together with an electric mixer on medium speed for about 30 seconds or until well combined. Beat in the vanilla and then the eggs one at a time until combined (about 30 seconds), scraping down the bowl and beaters as needed.

3. Reduce the mixer speed to low and slowly add the flour mixture, beating until combined (about 30 seconds). Give the dough a few final stirs with a rubber spatula to make sure it is well combined.

4. Working with two tablespoons at a time, roll the dough into balls with wet hands, then coat with the palm sugar. Place balls on the prepared baking sheets, spaced about two inches apart. Flatten the cookies to a three-quarter-inch thickness with the greased bottom of a drinking glass. Sprinkle the remaining palm sugar over the flat tops.

5. Bake the cookies, one sheet at a time, until the edges are set and beginning to brown, but the centers are still soft and puffy (10 to 12 minutes), rotating each baking sheet halfway through the baking. Cookies will spread out and flatten.

6. Let the cookies cool on the baking sheet for 10 minutes. Serve warm or transfer to a wire rack and cool completely.

Lime Sugar Cookies

MAKES 24 COOKIES

Ingredients

2 cups palm sugar

2½ cups almond flour

1 teaspoon lime zest, fresh grated

½ teaspoon baking powder

½ teaspoon salt

14 tablespoons coconut oil, softened

2 teaspoons vanilla extract

2 large eggs

2 teaspoons lime zest, fresh grated

Preparation

1. Adjust an oven rack to the middle position and heat the oven to 350°F. Line two large baking sheets with parchment paper. Process ½ cup palm sugar with one teaspoon grated lime zest in a food processor (about 10 seconds). Spread the ½ cup palm sugar and lime zest mixture in a shallow dish for rolling. In a medium bowl, whisk the flour, baking powder, and salt together.

2. In a separate large bowl, beat the coconut oil and remaining 1½ cups palm sugar together with an electric mixer on medium speed for about 30 seconds or until well combined. Beat in the vanilla, two teaspoons grated lime zest, and then the eggs one at a time until combined (about 30 seconds), scraping down the bowl and beaters as needed.

3. Reduce the mixer speed to low and slowly add the flour mixture, beating until combined (about 30 seconds). Give the dough a few final stirs with a rubber spatula to make sure it is well combined.

4. Working with two tablespoons at a time, roll the dough into balls with wet hands, then coat with the palm sugar. Place balls on the prepared baking sheets, spaced about three inches apart. Flatten the cookies to a three-quarter-inch thickness with the greased bottom of a drinking glass. Sprinkle the remaining palm sugar over the flat tops.

5. Bake the cookies, one sheet at a time, until the edges are set and beginning to brown, but the centers are still soft and puffy (10 to 12 minutes), rotating each baking sheet halfway through the baking. Cookies will spread out and flatten.

6. Let the cookies cool on the baking sheet for 10 minutes. Serve warm or transfer to a wire rack and cool completely.

Lemon Sugar Cookies

MAKES 24 COOKIES

Ingredients

2 cups palm sugar

2½ cups almond flour

3 teaspoons lemon zest, fresh grated, divided

½ teaspoon baking powder

½ teaspoon salt

14 tablespoons coconut oil, softened

2 teaspoons vanilla extract

2 large eggs

Preparation

1. Adjust an oven rack to the middle position and heat the oven to 350°F. Line two large baking sheets with parchment paper. Process ½ cup palm sugar with one teaspoon lemon zest in food processor until combined (about 10 seconds). Spread ½ cup of the palm sugar and lemon zest mixture in a shallow dish for rolling. In a medium bowl, whisk the flour, baking powder, and salt together.

2. In a large bowl, beat the coconut oil and remaining 1½ cups palm sugar together with an electric mixer on medium speed for about 30 seconds or until well combined. Beat in the vanilla, two teaspoons lemon zest, and then the eggs one at a time until combined (about 30 seconds), scraping down the bowl and beaters as needed.

3. Reduce the mixer speed to low and slowly add the flour mixture, beating until combined (about 30 seconds). Give the dough a few final stirs with a rubber spatula to make sure it is well combined.

4. Working with two tablespoons at a time, roll the dough into balls with wet hands, then coat with the palm sugar. Place balls on the prepared baking sheets, spaced about three inches apart. Flatten the cookies to a three-quarter-inch thickness with the greased bottom of a drinking glass. Sprinkle the remaining palm sugar over the flat tops.

5. Bake the cookies, one sheet at a time, until the edges are set and beginning to brown, but the centers are still soft and puffy (10 to 12 minutes), rotating each baking sheet halfway through the baking. Cookie will spread out and flatten.

6. Let the cookies cool on the baking sheet for 10 minutes. Serve warm or transfer to a wire rack and cool completely.

Molasses Spice Cookies

MAKES 24 COOKIES

Ingredients

⅔ cup palm sugar, divided

2¼ cups almond flour

1 teaspoon baking soda

1½ teaspoons ground cinnamon

1½ teaspoons ground ginger

½ teaspoon ground cloves

¼ teaspoon ground allspice

¼ teaspoon pepper

¼ teaspoon salt

5 tablespoons coconut oil, softened

1 large egg yolk

1 teaspoon vanilla extract

½ cup light or blackstrap molasses

Preparation

1. Adjust an oven rack to the middle position and heat the oven to 375°F. Line two baking sheets with parchment paper. Spread ⅓ cup of palm sugar into a shallow dish for rolling. In a medium bowl, whisk flour, baking soda, spices, pepper, and salt together.

2. In a separate large bowl, beat the coconut oil and remaining ⅓ cup palm sugar together with an electric mixer on medium speed for about 30 seconds or until well combined. Beat in the egg yolk and vanilla until combined (about 30 seconds). Beat in the molasses until incorporated (about 30 seconds), scraping down the bowl and beaters as needed.

3. Reduce the mixer speed to low and slowly add the flour mixture, beating until combined (about 30 seconds). The dough will be soft.

4. Working with two tablespoons at a time, roll the dough into balls with wet hands, then coat with the palm sugar. Place balls on the prepared baking sheets, spaced about two inches apart.

5. Bake the cookies, one sheet at a time, until the edges are set and beginning to brown, and the centers are still soft and puffy (10 to 12 minutes), rotating each baking sheet halfway through baking. (The cookies will look raw between the cracks and seem underdone.)

6. Let the cookies cool on the baking sheet for 10 minutes. Serve warm or transfer to a wire rack and cool completely.

Molasses Spice Cookies with Dark Rum Glaze

MAKES 24 COOKIES

Ingredients

⅔ cup palm sugar, divided

2¼ cups almond flour

1 teaspoon baking soda

1½ teaspoons ground cinnamon

1½ teaspoons ground ginger

½ teaspoon ground cloves

¼ teaspoon ground allspice

¼ teaspoon pepper

¼ teaspoon salt

5 tablespoons coconut oil, softened

1 large egg yolk

1 teaspoon vanilla extract

½ cup light or blackstrap molasses

Glaze

½ cup honey

3 tablespoons dark rum, or ½ teaspoon rum extract

Preparation

1. Adjust an oven rack to the middle position and heat the oven to 375°F. Line two baking sheets with parchment paper. Spread ⅓ cup palm sugar into a shallow dish for rolling. In a medium bowl, whisk flour, baking soda, spices, pepper, and salt together.

2. In a separate large bowl, beat the coconut oil and remaining ⅓ cup palm sugar together with an electric mixer on medium speed for about 30 seconds or until well combined. Beat in the egg yolk and vanilla until combined (about 30 seconds). Beat in the molasses until incorporated (about 30 seconds), scraping down the bowl and beaters as needed.

3. Reduce the mixer speed to low and slowly add the flour mixture, beating until combined (about 30 seconds). The dough will be soft.

4. Working with two tablespoons at a time, roll the dough into balls with wet hands, then coat with the palm sugar. Place balls on the prepared baking sheets, spaced about three inches apart.

5. Bake the cookies, one sheet at a time, until the edges are set and beginning to brown, and the centers are still soft and puffy (10 to 12 minutes), rotating each baking sheet halfway through baking. (The cookies will look raw between the cracks and seem underdone.)

6. Let the cookies cool on the baking sheet for 10 minutes. Serve warm or transfer to a wire rack and cool completely.

Making the Glaze

In a bowl, whisk together the honey and dark rum until well combined. Drizzle glaze over the cooled cookies and let sit for 10 to 15 minutes before serving.

Molasses Spice Cookies with Orange Essence

MAKES 24 COOKIES

Ingredients

1 cup palm sugar, divided

2 teaspoons orange zest, fresh grated

2¼ cups almond flour

1 teaspoon baking soda

1½ teaspoons ground cinnamon

1½ teaspoons ground ginger

½ teaspoon ground cloves

¼ teaspoon ground allspice

¼ teaspoon pepper

¼ teaspoon salt

5 tablespoons coconut oil, softened

1 large egg yolk

1 teaspoon vanilla extract

½ cup light or blackstrap molasses

1 teaspoon orange zest, fresh grated

Preparation

1. Adjust an oven rack to the middle position and heat the oven to 375°F. Line two baking sheets with parchment paper. Process ⅔ cup palm sugar with 2 teaspoons grated fresh orange zest in a food processor for about 10 seconds. Spread orange zest mixture into a shallow dish for rolling. In a medium bowl, whisk flour, baking soda, spices, pepper, and salt together.

2. In a separate large bowl, beat the coconut oil and ⅓ cup palm sugar together with an electric mixer on medium speed for about 30 seconds or until well combined. Beat in the egg yolk and vanilla until combined (about 30 seconds). Beat in the molasses and orange zest until incorporated (about 30 seconds), scraping down the bowl and beaters as needed.

3. Reduce the mixer speed to low and slowly add the flour mixture until combined (about 30 seconds). The dough will be soft.

4. Working with two tablespoons at a time, roll the dough into balls with wet hands, then coat with the palm sugar. Place balls on the prepared baking sheets, spaced about three inches apart.

5. Bake the cookies, one sheet at a time, until the edges are set and beginning to brown, and the centers are still soft and puffy (10 to 12 minutes), rotating each baking sheet halfway through baking. (The cookies will look raw between the cracks and seem underdone.)

6. Let the cookies cool on the baking sheet for 10 minutes. Serve warm or transfer to a wire rack and cool completely.

Lebkuchen

Ingredients

1¼ cups unblanched hazelnuts, toasted and cooled

1 cup unblanched whole almonds, toasted and cooled

¾ cup palm sugar

1½ teaspoons ground cinnamon

½ teaspoon ground cardamom

½ teaspoon nutmeg

3 tablespoons grated fresh orange zest

2 tablespoons grated fresh lemon zest

1½ cups almond flour

2 tablespoons cacao powder

½ teaspoon salt

6 tablespoons coconut oil, softened

¾ cup palm sugar

4 large eggs

1 teaspoon vanilla extract

Glaze

1 cup honey

¼ cup coconut milk

Preparation

1. Adjust the oven racks to the upper-middle and lower-middle positions and heat the oven to 350°F. Line two large baking sheets with parchment paper. Process the toasted nuts, palm sugar, cinnamon, cardamom, and nutmeg together into a fine meal using a food processor (about 30 to 60 seconds). Add the orange and lemon zest and continue to process until combined (about 15 seconds).

2. Whisk the flour, cacao powder, and salt together in a small bowl. In a large bowl, beat the coconut oil and the palm sugar together with an electric mixer on medium speed for about 30 seconds or until well combined. Beat in the eggs, one at a time, and vanilla, until combined, scraping down the bowl and beaters as needed.

3. Reduce the mixer speed to low and slowly add flour mixture, beating until combined (about 30 seconds). Mix in the ground nut mixture until just incorporated (the bowl will be very full).

4. Working with two tablespoons at a time, roll the dough into balls and lay them on the prepared baking sheets, spaced about two inches apart.

5. Bake the cookies until the edges are set and beginning to brown, and the centers are still soft and puffy with tiny cracks (13 to 18 minutes), switching and rotating

baking sheets halfway through baking. (The cookies will look raw between the cracks and seem underdone.)

6. Let the cookies cool on the baking sheet for 10 minutes. Transfer to a wire rack and cool completely. Repeat with remaining dough, using a freshly lined baking sheet.

Making the Glaze

When the cookies are cool, mix the honey and coconut milk together in a medium bowl until smooth. Using a pastry brush, brush a thin layer of the glaze over the tops of the cookies and let sit about 10 minutes before serving.

Jam Thumbprints

MAKES 48 COOKIES

Ingredients

½ cup raspberry jam (see Fruit Jam
  Recipe)

2¼ cups almond flour

8 tablespoons coconut flour

½ teaspoon salt

½ teaspoon baking soda

¼ teaspoon baking powder

12 tablespoons coconut oil, softened

⅔ cup palm sugar

3 ounces coconut milk

1 large egg

1½ teaspoons vanilla extract

Preparation

1. Adjust the oven racks to the upper-middle and lower-middle positions and heat the oven to 350°F. Line two baking sheets with parchment paper. Fill a small zipper seal bag with the jam. Whisk almond flour, coconut flour, salt, baking soda, and baking powder together in a medium bowl.

2. In a separate large bowl, beat the coconut oil and palm sugar together with an electric mixer on medium speed for about 30 seconds or until well combined. Beat in the coconut milk, eggs, and vanilla until combined (about 30 seconds), scraping down the bowl and beaters as necessary.

3. Reduce the mixer speed to low and slowly add the flour mixture, beating until combined (about 30 seconds).

4. Working with 1½ teaspoons at a time, roll the dough into balls and lay them on the prepared baking sheets, spaced about 1½ inches apart. Make an indention in the center of each cookie with your thumb.

5. Bake the cookies, one sheet at a time, until they are just beginning to set and are lightly browned around the edges (about 10 minutes). Remove the cookies from the oven and, working quickly, gently reshape the indention with the bottom of a teaspoon. Snip a small corner off the bag of jam and carefully fill each indention with about ½ teaspoon of the jam. Rotate the baking sheet and continue to bake until lightly golden and set, but not hard (12 to 14 minutes).

6. Let the cookies cool on the baking sheets for 10 minutes. Transfer to a wire rack and let cool completely (about 30 minutes) before serving.

Making Dough Ahead

The bowl of cookie dough can be wrapped tightly with plastic wrap and refrigerated for up to two days. When ready to use, allow the dough to come to room temperature, then portion and bake as directed. The dough can also be shaped into balls, marked with the thumbprint, and frozen on a cookie sheet. When they are frozen solid, transfer them to a large freezer bag. To bake, arrange the frozen cookies (do not thaw) on large parchment-lined baking sheets and bake about 15 minutes. Remove the cookies from the oven, reshape the indention as directed, fill with jam, and return to the oven to finish baking (14 to 19 minutes).

Almond Blossom Cookies

MAKES 48 COOKIES

Ingredients

1⅓ cups almond flour

½ cup dry roasted and salted almonds

¼ teaspoon baking soda

¼ teaspoon baking powder

¼ teaspoon salt

8 tablespoons coconut oil, softened

⅔ cup palm sugar

½ cup almond coconut oil

1 large egg

1 teaspoon vanilla extract

48 dark cacao nibs (Hershey's Kiss shape)

Preparation

1. Adjust an oven rack to the middle position and heat the oven to 350°F. Line two baking sheets with parchment paper. Process ⅔ cup of the almond flour and almonds together into a coarse meal using a food processor (about 15 seconds). Transfer the mixture to a medium bowl and stir in the remaining ⅔ cup almond flour, baking soda, baking powder, and salt.

2. In a separate large bowl, beat the coconut oil and palm sugar together with an electric mixer on medium-high speed until light and fluffy. Beat in the coconut oil, eggs, and vanilla until combined (about 30 seconds), scraping down the bowl and beaters as necessary.

3. Reduce the mixer speed to low and slowly add the flour mixture, beating until combined (about 30 seconds). Cover the bowl and refrigerate 30 minutes, or until the dough is stiff.

4. Working with 1½ teaspoons at a time, roll the dough into balls and lay them on baking sheets, spaced about 1½ inches apart.

5. Bake the cookies, one sheet at a time, until just set and beginning to crack (9 to 11 minutes), rotating each baking sheet halfway through baking. Working quickly, remove the cookies from the oven and firmly press one cacao nib in the center of each. Continue to bake the cookies until lightly golden, about 2 minutes longer.

6. Let the cookies cool on the baking sheet for 10 minutes. Transfer to a wire rack completely, (about two hours) before serving.

Making Dough Ahead

The bowl of cookie dough can be wrapped tightly with plastic wrap and refrigerated for up to two days. When ready to use, allow the dough to come to room temperature, then portion and bake as directed. The dough can also be shaped into balls and frozen on a cookie sheet. When they are frozen solid, transfer them to a large freezer bag. To bake, arrange the frozen cookies (do not thaw) on large parchment-lined baking sheets and bake as directed, increasing the baking time to 11 to 16 minutes before pressing the cacao nibs into the centers.

Chewy Chocolate Cookies

MAKES 24 COOKIES

Ingredients

1 cup coconut flour

1 cup cacao powder

½ teaspoon baking soda

¼ teaspoon salt

1½ cups palm sugar

4 large eggs

5 tablespoons coconut oil, melted and cooled slightly

1 teaspoon vanilla extract

2 ounces non-dairy bittersweet cacao nibs, finely chopped

Preparation

1. Adjust oven racks to upper-middle and lower-middle positions and heat oven to 375°F. Line two baking sheets with parchment paper. Whisk flour, cacao powder, baking soda, and salt together in bowl.

2. In a separate large bowl, whisk palm sugar, eggs, melted coconut oil, and vanilla together until well combined and smooth. Gently stir in flour mixture with rubber spatula until a soft dough forms. Stir in chopped cacao nibs.

3. Working with generous one-tablespoon portions, roll dough into balls using wet hands and place two inches apart on prepared sheets (12 cookies per sheet). Using the bottom of a slightly wet drinking glass, press cookies to a half-inch thickness.

4. Bake cookies until edges are just set, but centers are still soft and look underdone (10 to 12 minutes), switching and rotating sheets halfway through baking. Let cookies cool slightly on sheets. Serve warm or at room temperature.

Chocolate Chip Cookies

Ingredients

1 cup water	½ teaspoon salt
¼ cup finely chopped prunes or dates	1¼ cups palm sugar
3 tablespoons coconut oil	2 large eggs
2 cups almond flour	2 teaspoons vanilla extract
½ teaspoon baking soda	½ cup cacao nibs

Preparation

1. Bring water and prunes to a boil in a small saucepan over medium-high heat; reduce to a simmer and cook until prunes are tender and most of the water has evaporated (about 20 minutes). Using a rubber spatula, press the mixture through a fine-mesh strainer set over a bowl to make a date purée. Scrape any prunes left in strainer into the purée (you should have ¼ cup of purée).

2. Meanwhile, adjust oven rack to middle position; heat oven to 325°F. Line two baking sheets with parchment paper. Melt coconut oil in microwave for 30 seconds. Set aside.

3. Whisk flour, baking soda, and salt together in a bowl. Using a stand mixer fitted with a paddle beat prune purée, coconut oil, and palm sugar on medium speed until blended. Beat in egg and vanilla until combined. Reduce speed to low and beat in flour mixture until just incorporated. Give batter a final stir by hand, and then stir in all but two tablespoons of the cacao nibs.

4. Working with two tablespoons at a time, roll dough into balls, and press with fingers to create a cookie shape one-quarter-inch thick. Space cookies, torn side up, about two inches apart on prepared baking sheets (9 cookies per sheet). Press remaining two tablespoons of cacao nibs evenly into tops of cookies.

5. Bake cookies, one tray at a time, until edges are light golden brown and centers are soft and puffy (8 to 10 minutes) or until lightly browned, rotating sheet halfway through baking. Let cookies cool on sheet for 10 minutes, then serve warm or transfer to wire rack and cool completely.

Almond Butter Cookies

MAKES 24 COOKIES

Ingredients

1¼ cups almond flour

¾ teaspoon baking soda

½ teaspoon salt

½ cup creamy almond butter (no sugar or additives, all natural and fresh)

¾ cup palm sugar

⅓ cup honey

3 tablespoons coconut oil

2 large eggs

1 teaspoon vanilla extract

3 tablespoons unsalted almonds, chopped fine

Preparation

1. Adjust oven racks to upper-middle and lower-middle positions and heat oven to 350°F. Line two baking sheets with parchment paper. Whisk flour, baking soda, and salt together in a bowl.

2. In large bowl, whisk almond butter, honey, palm sugar, oil, melted coconut oil, egg, and vanilla together until smooth. Gently stir in flour mixture with rubber spatula until combined. Divide dough in half, wrap in plastic wrap, and refrigerate until firm, about one hour.

3. Working with two tablespoons at a time, roll dough into balls and place three inches apart on prepared sheets. Press dough to three-quarter-inch thickness using the bottom of a greased measuring cup. Press chopped almonds evenly into tops of cookies.

4. Bake cookies until puffed and edges are lightly browned (10 to 12 minutes), switching and rotating sheets halfway through baking. Let cookies cool on sheets for 10 minutes, then serve warm or transfer to wire rack to cool completely.

{ Icebox and Cookie Cutter Cookies }

Vanilla Icebox Cookies   43

Chocolate Icebox Cookies   44

Pine Nut-Raisin Icebox Cookies   47

Pecan Sandies   48

Thick and Chewy Gingerbread Cookies   51

Holiday Cookies   52

Jam Sandwiches   55

Vanilla Icebox Cookies

MAKES 48 COOKIES

Ingredients

2¼ cups almond flour

½ teaspoon salt

1 cup coconut oil, softened

1¼ cups palm sugar

2 large egg yolks

2 teaspoons vanilla extract

Preparation

1. Whisk flour and salt together in a medium bowl.
2. In a separate large bowl, beat the coconut oil and palm sugar together using an electric mixer on medium-high speed for about 30 seconds or until well combined. Beat in the egg yolks and vanilla until combined (about 30 seconds), scraping down the bowl and beaters as needed. Reduce the mixer speed to low and slowly add the flour mixture, beating until combined (about 30 seconds).
3. Transfer the dough to a clean counter and divide into two equal pieces. Roll each piece of dough into a six-inch-long log about two inches thick. Wrap the dough tightly in plastic wrap and refrigerate until firm, about two hours.
4. Twenty minutes before baking time, adjust the oven racks to the upper-middle and lower-middle positions and heat the oven to 325°F. Line two baking sheets with parchment paper.
5. Working with one log at a time, slice the dough into quarter-inch-thick cookies. Lay the cookies on the prepared baking sheets, spaced about ¾ inch apart. Bake the cookies until edges begin to brown (12 to 15 minutes), switching and rotating baking sheets halfway through baking.
6. Let the cookies cool on the baking sheets for 3 minutes, then transfer to a wire rack to cool completely before serving.

Chocolate Icebox Cookies

MAKES 48 COOKIES

Ingredients

2 cups almond flour

¼ cup cacao powder

½ teaspoon salt

1 cup coconut oil, softened

1¼ cup palm sugar

2 large egg yolks

2 teaspoons vanilla extract

2 ounces melted and cooled cacao nibs

Preparation

1. Whisk flour, cacao powder, and salt together in a medium bowl.
2. In a separate large bowl, beat the coconut oil and palm sugar together using an electric mixer on medium-high speed for about 30 seconds or until well combined. Beat in the egg yolks, melted cacao nibs, and vanilla until combined (about 30 seconds), scraping down the bowl and beaters as needed. Reduce the mixer speed to low and slowly add the flour mixture, beating until combined (about 30 seconds).
3. Transfer the dough to a clean counter and divide it into two equal pieces. Roll each piece of dough into a six-inch-long log, about two inches thick. Wrap the dough tightly in plastic wrap and refrigerate until firm, about two hours.
4. Adjust the oven racks to the upper-middle and lower-middle positions and heat the oven to 325°F. Line two baking sheets with parchment paper.
5. Working with one log at a time, slice the dough into quarter-inch-thick cookies. Lay the cookies on the prepared baking sheets, spaced about ¾ inch apart. Bake the cookies until edges begin to brown (12 to 15 minutes), switching and rotating baking sheets halfway through baking.
6. Let the cookies cool on the baking sheets for 3 minutes, then transfer to a wire rack to cool completely before serving.

Pine Nut-Raisin Icebox Cookies

MAKES 48 COOKIES

Ingredients

2¼ cups almond flour

¼ cup salted and toasted pine nuts or pistachios

¼ cup raisins

½ teaspoon salt

1 cup coconut oil, softened

1¼ cup palm sugar

2 large egg yolks

2 teaspoons vanilla extract

Preparation

1. Whisk flour, pine nuts, raisins, and salt together in a medium bowl.
2. In a separate large bowl, beat the coconut oil and palm sugar together using an electric mixer on medium-high speed for about 30 seconds or until well combined. Beat in the egg yolks and vanilla until combined (about 30 seconds), scraping down the bowl and beaters as needed. Reduce the mixer speed to low and slowly add the flour mixture, beating until combined (about 30 seconds). Fold in raisins and pine nuts with a spatula until evenly distributed.
3. Transfer the dough to a clean counter and divide it into two equal pieces. Roll each piece of dough into a six-inch-long log about two inches thick. Wrap the dough tightly in plastic wrap and refrigerate until firm, about two hours.
4. Adjust the oven racks to the upper-middle and lower-middle positions and heat the oven to 325°F. Line two baking sheets with parchment paper.
5. Working with one log at a time, slice the dough into quarter-inch-thick cookies. Lay the cookies on the prepared baking sheets, spaced about ¾ inch apart. Bake the cookies until edges begin to brown (12 to 15 minutes), switching and rotating baking sheets halfway through baking.
6. Let the cookies cool on the baking sheets for 3 minutes, then transfer to a wire rack to cool completely before serving.

Pecan Sandies

Ingredients

2 cups pecans, toasted
⅔ cup palm sugar
1½ cups almond flour
¼ teaspoon salt
12 tablespoons refrigerated coconut oil, cut into ½-inch pieces
1 large egg yolk

Preparation

1. Reserve 32 of the prettiest pecans for garnishing the cookies. Process the remaining 1½ cups pecans with the palm sugar in a food processor until the nuts are fully ground (about 20 seconds). Add the flour and salt and process to combine (about 10 seconds).

2. Add the coconut oil pieces and process until the mixture resembles damp sand and rides up the sides of the bowl (about 20 seconds). With the mixer running, add the egg yolk and process until the dough comes together into a rough ball (about 20 seconds).

3. Transfer the dough to a clean counter and divide into two equal pieces. Roll each piece of dough into a six-inch-long log about two inches thick. Wrap dough tightly in plastic wrap and refrigerate until firm, about two hours.

4. Adjust the oven racks to the upper-middle and lower-middle positions and heat the oven to 325°F. Line two large baking sheets with parchment paper.

5. Working with one log at a time, slice dough into half-inch-thick cookies. Place the cookies on the prepared baking sheets, spaced about one inch apart. Gently press a pecan half in the center of each cookie. Bake the cookies until the edges are golden brown (20 to 25 minutes), switching and rotating the baking sheets halfway through baking.

6. Let the cookies cool on the baking sheets for 3 minutes, then transfer to a wire rack to cool completely before serving.

Thick and Chewy Gingerbread Cookies

MAKES 20 GINGERBREAD PEOPLE OR 30 COOKIES

Ingredients

3 cups almond flour

¾ cup palm sugar

¾ teaspoon baking soda

1 tablespoon ground cinnamon

1 tablespoon ground ginger

½ teaspoon ground cloves

½ teaspoon salt

12 tablespoons coconut oil, softened

¾ cup blackstrap molasses

2 tablespoons coconut milk

Preparation

1. Process the flour, palm sugar, baking soda, cinnamon, ginger, cloves, and salt together in a food processor until combined (about 10 seconds). Add the coconut oil and process until the mixture is very fine and sandy (about 15 seconds). With the machine running, add the molasses and the coconut milk in a steady stream through the feed tube and continue to process until the dough comes together (about 10 seconds).

2. Divide the dough into two even pieces and roll each out to a quarter-inch thickness between two pieces of parchment paper. Leaving the dough sandwiched between parchments, stack them on a baking sheet and freeze until firm (15 to 20 minutes).

3. Adjust the oven racks to the upper-middle and lower-middle positions and heat the oven to 350°F. Line two large baking sheets with parchment paper.

4. Working with one piece of dough at a time, transfer dough to a clean counter and gently remove the top sheet of parchment. Stamp out cookies using cookie-cutters. Transfer the cookies to prepared baking sheets with a thin metal spatula, spaced about ¾ inch apart.

5. Bake the cookies until they are light golden brown and show a slight resistance to touch (8 to 11 minutes), switching and rotating the baking sheets halfway through baking. (Do not overbake.)

6. Let the cookies cool on the baking sheets for 3 minutes, then transfer to wire rack before serving.

Holiday Cookies

MAKES 18 COOKIES

Ingredients

2¼ cups almond flour

4 tablespoons coconut flour

¾ cup palm sugar

¼ teaspoon salt

16 tablespoons coconut oil, cut into ½-inch pieces and slightly softened

2 tablespoons coconut milk

1 teaspoon tapioca flour

2 teaspoons vanilla extract

Preparation

1. Place palm sugar in food processor and grind until superfine. Remove from processor and set aside in a bowl.

2. Whisk flour, palm sugar, tapioca flour, and salt together in a large bowl. Using an electric mixer on medium-low speed, beat the coconut oil into the flour mixture one piece at a time. Continue to beat the flour-coconut oil mixture until it looks crumbly and slightly wet.

3. Beat in the coconut milk and vanilla until the dough begins to form large clumps (about 30 seconds). Knead the dough in the bowl by hand a few times until it forms a large cohesive mass.

4. Transfer the dough to a clean counter and divide into two even pieces. Press each piece into a four-inch disc, wrap tightly in plastic wrap, and refrigerate until the dough is firm yet malleable (about 30 minutes).

5. Working with one piece of dough at a time, roll the dough out between two large sheets of parchment paper to an even quarter-inch thickness. With the dough sandwiched between the parchments, slide it onto a baking sheet and refrigerate until firm (about 10 minutes).

6. Adjust an oven rack to the middle position and heat the oven to 375°F. Line two baking sheets with parchment paper.

7. Working with one sheet of dough at a time, remove the top piece of parchment and stamp out cookies using cookie cutters. Transfer the cookies to the prepared baking sheet with a thin metal spatula, spaced about one inch apart.

8. Bake the cookies one sheet at a time until light golden brown (about 10 minutes), rotating the baking sheets halfway through baking. Let the cookies cool on the baking sheet for 3 minutes, then transfer to a wire rack to cool completely before decorating as desired. Repeat with the remaining dough using freshly lined baking sheets.

DECORATING GLAZES: Use your favorite paleo jams (see Fruit Jam Recipe, page 221) as a glaze to decorate, or pipe non-dairy dark, milk, or white cacao nibs. Cacao decorating glaze can be made smooth by adding a small amount of coconut oil and coconut milk while heating to reach desired consistency. Heat cacao nibs in microwave, stirring every 30 seconds until smooth.

Jam Sandwiches

MAKES 30 COOKIES

Ingredients

1 recipe Holiday Cookie Dough, prepared through step five

1¼ cups favorite paleo jam (see Fruit Jam Recipe, page 221)

2 tablespoons palm sugar, finely processed

Preparation

1. While the sheets of Holiday Cookie Dough chill, simmer the jam in a small saucepan over medium heat until it is thickened and measures one cup (about 20 minutes). Strain the jam, discarding the solids, and set aside to cool. Adjust the oven racks to the upper-middle and lower-middle positions and heat the oven to 375°F. Line two large baking sheets with parchment paper.

2. Remove the top piece of parchment from one of the sheets of dough and stamp out cookies with a two-inch, round-fluted cookie cutter. Lay the cookies on the prepared baking sheets, spaced about one inch apart.

3. Bake the cookies until the edges begin to brown (12 to 15 minutes), switching and rotating the baking sheets halfway through baking. Let the cookies cool on the baking sheets for 3 minutes, then, using a wide metal spatula, transfer them to a wire rack to cool completely. Cool the baking sheets and line with fresh parchment paper.

4. Meanwhile, remove the top piece of parchment from the remaining sheet of dough and sprinkle with the palm sugar. Stamp out cookies with a two-inch, round-fluted cookie cutter and then stamp out the center of each using a three-quarter-inch, round cookie cutter. Bake and cool the cookies as directed in step three.

5. When the cookies are cool, spread one teaspoon of the cooked jam over each solid cookie, then top with a cutout cookie and press lightly to adhere. Serve cookies immediately after adding jam as they will soften and may break apart if allowed to sit for too long.

{ Brownies and Bars Cookies }

Lunch Box Brownies   59   Blondies   75

Fudgy Brownies   60   Almond Fudge Bars   76

Whoopie Pies   63   Peach Squares   78

Vanilla Pudding Bars   64   Apricot Squares   80

Pecan Bars   66   Strawberry Squares   82

Raspberry Streusel Bars   68   Fig Bars   84

Lemon Squares   71   Paleo Marshmallows   87

Key Lime Bars   72

Lunchbox Brownies

MAKES 16 BROWNIES

Ingredients

8 tablespoons coconut oil

3 ounces cacao nibs

⅔ cup almond flour

½ teaspoon baking powder

¼ teaspoon salt

1 cup palm sugar

2 large eggs

1 teaspoon vanilla extract

½ cup pecans or walnuts, toasted and chopped

Coconut oil for greasing foil

Preparation

1. Adjust oven rack to the middle position and heat the oven to 350°F. Line an eight-inch square baking pan with a foil sling and grease foil with coconut oil. Heat 8 tablespoons coconut oil and cacao nibs together in the microwave, stirring often, for 1 to 3 minutes or until melted. Let the mixture cool slightly.

2. In a medium bowl, whisk together the flour, baking powder, and salt. In a separate large bowl, whisk together the palm sugar, eggs, and vanilla. Whisk in the melted cacao nibs mixture until combined. Stir in the flour mixture until just incorporated.

3. Scrape the batter into the prepared pan, smooth the top, and sprinkle with the toasted nuts. Bake the brownies until a toothpick inserted into the center comes out with just a few moist crumbs attached (22 to 27 minutes), rotating the pan halfway through baking.

4. Let the brownies cool completely in the pan, set on a wire rack (about two hours). Cut the brownies into squares, remove from the pan, and serve.

Fudgy Brownies

Serves 16

Ingredients

---

2 ounces cacao nibs, chopped

2 tablespoons coconut oil

¾ cup coconut flour

⅓ cup cacao powder

½ teaspoon baking powder

¼ teaspoon kosher salt

1 cup palm sugar

2 tablespoons coconut milk

2 large eggs

2 teaspoons vanilla extract

Coconut oil for greasing foil

Preparation

1. Adjust oven rack to the middle position and preheat oven to 350°F. Make foil sling for eight-inch square baking pan by folding two long sheets of aluminum foil so that each is eight inches wide. Lay sheets of foil in pan perpendicular to each other, with extra foil hanging over edges of pan. Push foil into corners and up sides of pan, smoothing foil flush to pan. Grease foil with coconut oil.

2. Microwave cacao nibs and coconut oil together in covered bowl, stirring occasionally, until melted and smooth (1 to 3 minutes). Transfer to large bowl and cool slightly. In a separate bowl, whisk flour, cacao powder, baking powder, and salt together.

3. Whisk palm sugar, coconut milk, eggs, and vanilla into melted cacao nibs. Fold in flour mixture until just incorporated. Scrape batter into prepared pan and smooth top.

4. Bake brownies until a toothpick inserted in center comes out with few moist crumbs attached (20 to 25 minutes), rotating pan halfway through baking. Let brownies cool completely in pan on wire rack, about two hours. Remove brownies from pan using foil sling, cut into sixteen squares, and serve.

Whoopie Pies

SERVES 8

Ingredients

1 cup cacao powder

1 cup warm tap water

1½ cups almond flour

½ teaspoon baking soda

¼ teaspoon salt

1 cup palm sugar

5 tablespoons coconut oil, melted and
cooled

1¼ teaspoons vanilla extract

2 large eggs

2 ounces coconut milk

1 teaspoon tapioca flour

4 tablespoons white chocolate chips

¼ Vanilla Pudding Recipe (page 203)

Preparation

1. Adjust oven racks to upper-middle and lower-middle positions and preheat oven to 375°F. Line two baking sheets with parchment paper. Whisk cacao powder and water together in bowl. In a separate bowl, whisk flour, baking soda, and salt together.

2. In large bowl, whisk palm sugar, coconut oil, and one teaspoon vanilla together until incorporated. Whisk in eggs and cacao powder mixture until smooth. Gently stir in flour mixture with a rubber spatula until a soft dough forms.

3. Using a greased quarter-cup measure, drop scant quarter-cup scoops of batter two inches apart on prepared baking sheets (you should have sixteen cakes total). Bake cakes until toothpick inserted in center comes out clean (about 14 minutes), switching and rotating sheets halfway through baking. Let cakes cool completely on sheets.

Filling

Use a quarter of the recipe for Vanilla Pudding to fill the Whoopie Pies. Assemble eight sandwich cookies by spreading about two tablespoons of filling between two cookies. Serve.

Vanilla Pudding Bars

SERVES 16

Ingredients

Crust

1½ cups almond flour

3 tablespoons coconut oil, melted and
  cooled

3 tablespoons palm sugar

⅓ teaspoon salt

Filling and Topping

2 cups coconut milk

4 tablespoons tapioca flour

⅔ cup honey

2 teaspoons lemon juice

1 teaspoon vanilla extract

2 large eggs

5 small strawberries, hulled and sliced thin

Coconut oil for greasing foil

Preparation

1. Adjust oven rack to middle position and preheat oven to 350°F. Make a foil sling
   for an eight-inch square baking pan by folding two long sheets of aluminum foil
   so each is eight inches wide. Lay sheets of foil in pan perpendicular to each other,
   with extra foil hanging over edges of pan. Push foil into corners and up sides of
   pan, smoothing foil flush to pan. Grease foil with coconut oil.

2. Place almond flour in a food processor and process to fine, even crumbs (about 30
   seconds). Add melted coconut oil, palm sugar, and salt and pulse to incorporate,
   about five pulses. Transfer mixture to prepared pan and press firmly into an even
   layer using a wide metal spatula. Bake until crust is fragrant and beginning to
   brown (12 to 15 minutes), rotating pan halfway through baking. Let cool on wire
   rack for at least 15 minutes.

3. Add coconut milk, palm sugar, tapioca flour to a bowl and whisk to combine.
   Add palm sugar mixture and whisk to combine. Transfer mixture to a saucepan
   and bring to a boil over high heat, whisking constantly. Reduce heat to medium-
   high and whisk until thick and glossy (1-2 minutes).

4. Pour pudding mixture over cooled crust. Allow to cool at room temperature
   for 10 minutes. Cover loosely with plastic wrap and refrigerate until thoroughly
   chilled (at least three hours). Remove from the pan using the foil sling and cut
   into sixteen squares. For thicker bars, stack one square on top of another and
   garnish each with a strawberry slice or mint leaf before serving.

Pecan Bars

Ingredients

Crust

¾ cup almond flour

⅓ cup palm sugar

¼ cup pecans, toasted and chopped coarse

¼ teaspoon salt

¼ teaspoon baking powder

3 tablespoons coconut oil—more if needed to moisten

½ tablespoon water

Filling

⅓ cup palm sugar

⅓ cup honey

2 tablespoons coconut oil, melted

1 tablespoon bourbon or dark rum or ½ teaspoon rum extract

2 teaspoons vanilla extract

¼ teaspoon salt

1 large egg

¾ cup pecans, chopped coarse

Coconut oil for greasing foil

Preparation

1. Adjust oven rack to middle position and preheat oven to 350°F. Make a foil sling for an eight-inch square baking pan by folding two long sheets of aluminum foil so each is eight inches wide. Lay sheets of foil in pan perpendicular to each other, with extra foil hanging over edges of pan. Push foil into corners and up sides of pan, smoothing foil flush to pan. Grease foil with coconut oil.

2. Pulse flour, palm sugar, pecans, salt, and baking powder together in a food processor until combined (about five pulses). Sprinkle coconut oil over top, add ½ tablespoon of water, and pulse until mixture is pale yellow and resembles coarse cornmeal (about eight pulses). Transfer mixture to prepared pan and press firmly into an even layer using a wide metal spatula. Bake until crust is fragrant and beginning to brown (about 20 minutes), rotating pan halfway through baking. Let cool on wire rack for at least 15 minutes.

3. Whisk palm sugar, honey, coconut oil, bourbon, vanilla, egg, and salt together in a saucepan over medium heat until palm sugar dissolves. Stir in pecans. Spread filling evenly over crust. Bake until top is golden brown (22 to 25 minutes), rotating pan halfway through baking.
4. Let bars cool completely in pan on wire rack for about two hours. Remove from pan using foil sling and cut into sixteen squares. Serve.

Raspberry Streusel Bars

Ingredients

Crust

¾ cup almond flour

⅓ cup packed palm sugar

¼ cup pecans, toasted and chopped coarse

½ teaspoon salt

¼ teaspoon baking powder

3 tablespoons coconut oil

Filling

¾ cup raspberry jam
   (see Fruit Jam recipe)

2½ ounces raspberries

1 tablespoon lemon juice

½ cup almond meal

¼ cup palm sugar

2 tablespoons coconut flour

¼ teaspoon ground cinnamon

⅓ teaspoon salt

2 tablespoons coconut oil

Coconut oil for greasing foil

Preparation

1. Adjust oven rack to middle position and preheat oven to 350°F. Make a foil sling for an eight-inch square baking pan by folding two long sheets of aluminum foil so each is eight inches wide. Lay sheets of foil in pan perpendicular to each other, with extra foil hanging over edges of pan. Push foil into corners and up sides of pan, smoothing foil flush to pan. Grease foil with coconut oil.

2. Pulse flour, palm sugar, pecans, salt, and baking powder in a food processor until combined (about 5 pulses). Sprinkle coconut oil over top and pulse until mixture resembles coarse cornmeal (about 8 pulses). Transfer mixture to prepared pan and press firmly into an even layer using wide metal spatula. Bake until crust is fragrant and beginning to brown (20 to 24 minutes), rotating pan halfway through baking. Let cool on wire rack for at least 15 minutes.

3. Increase the oven temperature to 375°F. Mash jam, raspberries, and lemon juice together in a bowl with a fork until just a few pieces of raspberry remain. In a separate bowl, combine almond meal, palm sugar, flour, cinnamon, and salt, then add melted coconut oil and toss gently with a fork. Spread berry mixture

evenly over baked crust, then sprinkle with almond meal mixture. Bake bars until filling is bubbling and topping is deep golden brown (22 to 25 minutes), rotating pan halfway through baking.

4. Let bars cool completely in pan on wire rack for about two hours. Remove from pan using foil sling and cut into sixteen squares. Serve.

Lemon Squares

Ingredients

Crust

¾ cup coconut flour

⅓ cup palm sugar

3 tablespoons tapioca flour

1 teaspoon grated lemon zest

½ teaspoon baking powder

¼ teaspoon salt

4 tablespoons coconut oil

1 tablespoon coconut milk

Filling

1½ cups palm sugar

2 large eggs, plus 2 large egg whites

4 tablespoons coconut flour

⅔ teaspoon salt

2 tablespoons grated lemon zest

12 tablespoons lemon juice (4 lemons)

2 tablespoons palm sugar

Coconut oil for greasing foil

Preparation

1. Adjust oven rack to middle position and preheat oven to 350°F. Make a foil sling for an eight-inch square baking pan by folding two long sheets of aluminum foil so each is eight inches wide. Lay sheets of foil in pan perpendicular to each other, with extra foil hanging over edges of pan. Push foil into corners and up sides of pan, smoothing foil flush to pan. Grease with coconut oil.

2. Process flour, palm sugar, tapioca flour, lemon zest, baking powder, and salt in a food processor until combined (about 10 seconds). Add coconut oil and coconut milk and pulse until mixture resembles coarse meal (about 10 pulses). Transfer mixture to prepared pan and press firmly into an even layer using a wide metal spatula. Bake until edges are lightly browned (16 to 20 minutes), rotating pan halfway through baking. Let cool on wire rack for at least 15 minutes.

3. Reduce oven temperature to 325°F. Whisk palm sugar, eggs, egg whites, flour, and salt together in bowl until smooth. Stir in lemon zest and juice. Pour filling over baked crust. Bake until filling is set (15 to 20 minutes). Let bars cool completely in pan on wire rack for about one hour.

4. Remove from pan using foil sling, cut into nine squares, and sprinkle with palm sugar. Serve.

Key Lime Bars

Serves 16

Ingredients

Crust

2½ cups almond flour

4 tablespoons coconut oil, melted

3 tablespoons palm sugar

1 pinch salt

Filling

2 ounces coconut milk

2 teaspoons tapioca flour

1 tablespoon grated lime zest, plus ½ cup lime juice (4 limes)

1 pinch salt

7 ounces coconut milk

7 ounces honey

1 large egg white

Coconut oil for greasing foil

Preparation

1. Adjust oven rack to middle position and preheat oven to 325°F. Make a foil sling for an eight-inch square baking pan by folding two long sheets of aluminum foil so each is eight inches wide. Lay sheets of foil in pan perpendicular to each other, with extra foil hanging over edges of pan. Push foil into corners and up sides of pan, smoothing foil flush to pan. Grease with coconut oil.

2. Process almond flour in a food processor to fine, even crumbs (about 30 seconds). Add melted coconut oil, palm sugar, and salt and pulse to incorporate (about 5 pulses). Transfer mixture to prepared pan and press firmly into an even layer using a wide metal spatula. Bake until crust is fragrant and beginning to brown (12 to 16 minutes), rotating pan halfway through baking. Let cool on wire rack for at least 15 minutes.

3. Combine coconut milk, tapioca flour, lime zest, and salt in medium bowl. Whisk in 7 ounces of coconut milk and honey until smooth, then whisk in the egg white, followed by the lime juice. Pour filling over baked crust and smooth the top. Bake until the center is firm and edges begin to pull away slightly from sides (15 to 20 minutes).

4. Let bars cool completely in pan on wire rack for about one hour. Cover loosely with plastic wrap and refrigerate until thoroughly chilled (2 to 3 hours). Remove from pan using foil sling and cut into sixteen squares. Serve.

Blondies

SERVES 24

Ingredients

1½ cups honey

2 tablespoons coconut oil, melted

½ teaspoon salt

1 teaspoon baking powder

2 large eggs

2 teaspoons vanilla extract

1¼ cups coconut flour

½ cup cacao nibs

⅓ cup dairy-free white chocolate chips

Coconut for greasing foil

Preparation

1. Adjust oven rack to middle position and preheat oven to 350°F. Make a foil sling for a 13x9 baking pan by folding two long sheets of aluminum foil; the first sheet should be thirteen inches wide and the second sheet should be nine inches wide. Lay sheets of foil in pan perpendicular to each other, with extra foil hanging over edges of pan. Push foil into corners and up sides of pan, smoothing foil flush to pan. Grease foil with coconut oil.

2. Whisk honey, melted coconut oil, and salt together in a large bowl. Whisk in eggs and vanilla until no lumps remain and mixture is thick, smooth, and shiny. Gently stir in flour with a rubber spatula until combined.

3. Scrape batter into prepared pan, smooth top, and sprinkle with white and cacao nibs. Bake until a toothpick inserted into center comes out with few moist crumbs attached (22 to 25 minutes), rotating pan halfway through baking.

4. Place the pan atop a wire rack and let the blondies cool completely (about two hours). Remove the bars from the pan using the foil, cut into squares, and serve.

Almond Fudge Bars

Ingredients

Crust and Topping

½ cup almond flour

½ cup almond meal

⅓ cup palm sugar

¼ teaspoon baking powder

⅓ teaspoon salt

4 tablespoons coconut oil, melted and
    cooled

Filling

½ cup coconut flour

1½ teaspoons instant espresso powder or
    instant coffee powder

¼ teaspoon salt

1 cup cacao nibs

4 ounces paleo marshmallows (see Paleo
    Marshmallow recipe, page 87)

¼ cup coconut milk

1 teaspoon vanilla extract

Coconut oil to grease the foil sling

Preparation

1. Adjust oven rack to middle position and preheat oven to 325°F. Make a foil sling for eight-inch square baking pan by folding two long sheets of aluminum foil so each is eight inches wide. Lay sheets of foil in pan perpendicular to each other, with extra foil hanging over edges of pan. Push foil into corners and up sides of pan, smoothing foil flush to pan. Grease foil with coconut oil.

2. Whisk almond flour, almond meal, palm sugar, baking powder, and salt together in bowl. Stir in melted coconut oil until combined. Measure out and reserve ¼ cup of mixture for topping. Transfer remaining mixture to prepared pan and press firmly into an even layer using a wide metal spatula. Bake crust until fragrant and beginning to brown (20 to 24 minutes), rotating pan halfway through baking. Let cool on wire rack for at least 15 minutes.

3. Whisk coconut flour, espresso powder, and salt together in a bowl. Microwave cacao nibs, marshmallows, and coconut milk together in a large bowl, stirring

often, until melted and smooth, about 1 to 3 minutes. Allow mixture to cool slightly, then stir in vanilla and flour mixture until just incorporated.

4. Spread filling evenly over baked crust. Sprinkle with reserved almond flour/ meal mixture and spray lightly with vegetable oil spray. Bake until edges are set but center is still slightly soft (about 20 minutes), rotating pan halfway through baking.

5. Place the pan atop a wire rack and let the bars cool completely (about two hours). Remove the bars from the pan using the foil, cut into squares, and serve.

Peach Squares

MAKES 24 SQUARES

Ingredients

1½ cups almond flour

1¾ cups sliced almonds

⅔ cup palm sugar + 1 tablespoon palm sugar

1 pinch salt

6 tablespoons coconut oil, cut into 12 pieces and softened

1½ pounds frozen peaches, thawed and drained

½ cup peach jam (see Fruit Jam recipe)

½ teaspoon grated fresh lemon zest

1 teaspoon fresh lemon juice

Coconut oil for greasing foil

Preparation

1. Adjust an oven rack to the middle position and preheat the oven to 375°F. Line a 13x9 baking pan with a foil sling. Make foil sling by folding two long sheets of aluminum foil; the first sheet should be thirteen inches wide and the second sheet should be nine inches wide. Lay sheets of foil in pan perpendicular to each other, with extra foil hanging over edges of pan. Push foil into corners and up sides of pan, smoothing foil flush to pan. Grease with coconut oil.

2. Process the flour, 1¼ cups of the almonds, ⅓ cup of the palm sugar, and ½ teaspoon salt together in a food processor until combined (about 5 seconds). Add the coconut oil and pulse until the mixture resembles coarse meal, with a few pea-sized pieces of coconut oil (about 20 pulses).

3. Reserve ½ cup of the flour mixture for the topping. Sprinkle the remaining flour mixture into the prepared pan and press into an even layer with the bottom of a measuring cup. Bake the crust until fragrant and golden brown (about 15 minutes).

4. While the crust bakes, mix the remaining tablespoon of palm sugar and the reserved flour mixture together in a small bowl and pinch the mixture between your fingers into hazelnut-sized clumps of streusel.

5. Pulse the peaches and jam together in a food processor until the peaches are roughly quarter-inch chunks (5 to 7 pulses). Cook the peach mixture in a large nonstick skillet over high heat until it is thickened and jam-like (10 minutes). Remove from heat and stir in lemon zest, lemon juice, and a pinch of salt.

6. Spread the cooked peach mixture evenly over the hot crust and sprinkle with the streusel topping and remaining ½ cup of almonds. Bake until almonds are golden brown (about 20 minutes), rotating the pan halfway through baking.
7. Place the pan atop a wire rack and let the bars cool completely (about two hours). Remove the bars from the pan using the foil, cut into squares, and serve.

Apricot Squares

Ingredients

1½ cups almond flour

1¾ cups sliced almonds

⅔ cup palm sugar + 1 tablespoon palm
   sugar

1 pinch salt

6 tablespoons coconut oil, cut into 12
   pieces and softened

1 pound dried apricots

½ cup apricot jam (see Fruit Jam recipe,
   page 221)

1 cup of water

½ teaspoon grated fresh lemon zest

1 teaspoon fresh lemon juice

Coconut oil for greasing foil

Preparation

1. Adjust an oven rack to the middle position and preheat the oven to 375°F. Line a 13x9 baking pan with a foil sling. Make foil sling by folding two long sheets of aluminum foil; the first sheet should be thirteen inches wide and the second sheet should be nine inches wide. Lay sheets of foil in pan perpendicular to each other, with extra foil hanging over edges of pan. Push foil into corners and up sides of pan, smoothing foil flush to pan. Grease with coconut oil.

2. Process the flour, 1¼ cups of the almonds, ⅓ cup of the palm sugar, and ½ teaspoon salt together in a food processor until combined (about 5 seconds). Add the coconut oil and pulse until the mixture resembles coarse meal, with a few pea-sized pieces of coconut oil (about 20 pulses).

3. Reserve ½ cup of the flour mixture for the topping. Sprinkle the remaining flour mixture into the prepared pan and press into an even layer with the bottom of a measuring cup. Bake the crust until fragrant and golden brown (about 15 minutes).

4. While the crust bakes, mix the remaining 1 tablespoon of palm sugar and the reserved flour mixture together in a small bowl and pinch the mixture between your fingers into hazelnut-sized clumps of streusel.

5. Pulse the apricots, one cup of water, and jam together in a food processor until the apricots are roughly quarter-inch chunks (5 to 7 pulses). Cook the apricot mixture in a large nonstick skillet over high heat until it is thickened and jam-like (10 minutes). Remove from heat and stir in lemon zest, lemon juice, and a pinch of salt.

6. Spread the cooked apricot mixture evenly over the hot crust and sprinkle with the streusel topping and remaining ½ cup of almonds. Bake until almonds are golden brown (about 20 minutes), rotating the pan halfway through baking.
7. Place the pan atop a wire rack and let the bars cool completely (about two hours). Remove the bars from the pan using the foil, cut into squares, and serve.

Strawberry Squares

Ingredients

1½ cups almond flour

1¾ cups sliced almonds

⅔ cup + 1 tablespoon palm sugar

1 pinch salt

12 tablespoons coconut oil, cut into
   12 pieces and softened

1½ pounds strawberries

½ cup strawberry jam
   (see Fruit Jam recipe, page 221)

1 cup of water

½ teaspoon grated fresh lemon zest

½ teaspoon fresh lemon juice

¼ teaspoon vanilla extract

Coconut oil for greasing foil

Preparation

1. Adjust an oven rack to the middle position and preheat the oven to 375°F. Line a 13x9 baking pan with a foil sling. Make foil sling by folding two long sheets of aluminum foil; the first sheet should be thirteen inches wide and the second sheet should be nine inches wide. Lay sheets of foil in pan perpendicular to each other, with extra foil hanging over edges of pan. Push foil into corners and up sides of pan, smoothing foil flush to pan. Grease with coconut oil.

2. Process the flour, 1¼ cups of the almonds, ⅓ cup of the palm sugar, and ½ teaspoon salt together in a food processor until combined (about 5 seconds). Add the coconut oil and pulse until the mixture resembles coarse meal, with a few pea-sized pieces of coconut oil (about 20 pulses).

3. Reserve ½ cup of the flour mixture for the topping. Sprinkle the remaining flour mixture into the prepared pan and press into an even layer with the bottom of a measuring cup. Bake the crust until fragrant and golden brown (about 15 minutes).

4. While the crust bakes, mix the remaining tablespoon of palm sugar and the reserved flour mixture together in a small bowl and pinch the mixture between your fingers into hazelnut-sized clumps of streusel.

5. Pulse the strawberries, vanilla extract, and jam together in a food processor until the strawberries are roughly quarter-inch chunks (5 to 7 pulses). Cook the

strawberry mixture in a large nonstick skillet over high heat until it is thickened and jam-like (10 minutes). Remove from heat and stir in lemon zest, lemon juice, and a pinch of salt.

6. Spread the cooked strawberry mixture evenly over the hot crust and sprinkle with the streusel topping and remaining ½ cup of almonds. Bake until almonds are golden brown (about 20 minutes), rotating the pan halfway through baking.

7. Place the pan atop a wire rack and let the bars cool completely (about two hours). Remove the bars from the pan using the foil, cut into squares, and serve.

Fig Bars

MAKES 16 BARS

Ingredients

Filling

8 ounces dried Turkish or Calimyrna Figs, stemmed and quartered

2 cups apple cider

1 pinch salt

2 teaspoons fresh lemon juice

Crust

¾ cup almond flour

½ cup coconut flour

½ teaspoon baking powder

¼ teaspoon salt

6 tablespoons coconut oil, softened

¾ cup palm sugar

2 large eggs

2 teaspoons vanilla extract

Coconut oil for greasing foil

Preparation

1. Simmer the figs, apple juice, and salt in a medium saucepan over medium heat, stirring occasionally until the figs are very soft and the liquid is syrupy (15 to 20 minutes). Allow the mixture to cool slightly. Purée the figs in a food processor with the lemon juice until the mixture has a thick jam consistency (about 8 seconds).

2. Adjust an oven rack to the middle position and preheat the oven to 350°F. Line an eight-inch square baking pan with a foil sling. Make a foil sling for an eight-inch square baking pan by folding two long sheets of aluminum foil so each is eight inches wide. Lay sheets of foil in pan perpendicular to each other, with extra foil hanging over edges of pan. Push foil into corners and up sides of pan, smoothing foil flush to pan. Grease foil with coconut oil.

3. Whisk flours, baking powder, and salt together in a medium bowl.

4. In a large bowl, beat the coconut oil and palm sugar together with an electric mixer on medium speed until light and fluffy (3 to 6 minutes). Beat the egg and vanilla until combined. Stir in the flour mixture until just incorporated. Reserve ¾ cup of the dough for topping.

5. Sprinkle the remaining mixture into the prepared pan and press into an even layer with the greased spatula. Top with a piece of greased parchment and smooth into an even layer with the bottom of a measuring cup. Remove the parchment and bake the crust until just beginning to turn golden (about 20 minutes).

6. Meanwhile, roll the reserved dough for the top crust between two sheets of greased parchment paper into an eight-inch square; turn the edges of the dough as needed to measure exactly eight inches. Leaving the dough sandwiched between the parchment, transfer to a baking sheet, and place it in the freezer until needed.

7. Spread the fig mixture evenly over the baked crust. Unwrap the frozen, reserved top crust and lay it over the filling, pressing lightly to adhere. Bake the bars until the top crust is golden brown (25 to 30 minutes), rotating the pan halfway through baking.

8. Place the pan atop a wire rack and let the fig bars cool completely (about two hours). Remove the bars from the pan using the foil, cut into squares, and serve.

Paleo Marshmallows

MAKES AN 8X8 PAN OF MARSHMALLOWS

Ingredients

1 cup water (divided into 2½ cups)

3 tablespoons grass-fed beef gelatin

1 cup honey

1 teaspoon vanilla extract

¼ teaspoon salt

Coconut oil

Tapioca flour to coat the outside of the
marshmallows

Coconut oil for greasing foil

Preparation

1. Make a foil sling for an eight-inch square baking pan by folding two long sheets of aluminum foil so each is eight inches wide. Lay sheets of foil in pan perpendicular to each other, with extra foil hanging over edges of pan. Push foil into corners and up sides of pan, smoothing foil flush to pan. Grease foil with coconut oil and sprinkle with a thin layer of tapioca flour.

2. Add gelatin and ½ cup of the water to the bowl of a stand mixer.

3. While the gelatin is softening, add remaining ½ cup of water, honey, and salt into a saucepan over medium heat. Bring the mixture to a boil. Place a candy thermometer in the saucepan and continue to boil the mixture until it reaches 242°F, the soft ball stage. Don't exceed 245°F.

NOTE If you're making these at higher elevation, decrease the cooking temperature by 2°F per 1,000 feet. If your pot is too big, the palm sugar syrup will be more likely to burn, as the temperature will rise too quickly and the thermometer may not read accurately. If the honey mixture foams, use a spoon to break up the foam so that it doesn't overflow, but do not stir the syrup.

4. When palm sugar mixture reaches 240-242°F, immediately remove the saucepan from the heat.

5. Turn the stand mixer on low-medium speed and begin mixing the gelatin and water. Pour the honey mixture in a slow, steady stream down the side of the bowl, not pouring directly on the gelatin. It's critical to pour in this manner to prevent

the hot palm sugar mixture from "breaking" the gelatin, which will cause the marshmallow mixture to break up later when it's time to spread and form.

6. When the syrup and the gelatin are well combined, turn off the mixer and, using a spoon, give it a final stir.

7. Turn the mixer speed to high and continue beating until mixture cools and becomes very thick, like marshmallow crème (7 to 10 minutes). Add vanilla during the last minute of mixing.

8. Transfer the marshmallow crème to the prepared pan with foil sling. Smooth the top.

9. Allow the marshmallows to stand at room temperature for one to six hours until they reach the desired firmness. If you want a clean look after cutting, wait at least four hours before cutting. Even if you think they are firm enough, wait!

10. Remove from pan using foil sling and fold down sides of foil. Cut marshmallows to the desired size, adding more tapioca flour while cutting to keep knife from sticking. Toss again in tapioca flour when finished to give them a nice finish.

11. Using tapioca flour works well for coating marshmallows that will be used for roasting or topping dishes. It enables quicker drying times and aids in the browning process. Marshmallows intended for roasting should be cut and left at room temperature overnight, covered with cheesecloth. Then store the marshmallows in a sealed container in the refrigerator for five to seven days, or until needed.

Other coating and dipping options

Try all kinds of crushed nuts, coconut, almond flour mixed with spices, cacao powder, or other starches. If you want to dip the marshmallows in cacao nibs, melt your cacao nibs of choice, allow to cool slightly, and either dip the bottoms or drizzle the melted cacao nibs on top. Stick in the fridge for about 5 minutes to let the cacao nibs harden, and then store as instructed above.

{ Snack Cakes, Sheet Cakes, Bundt Cakes, and Cupcakes }

Applesauce Snack Cake	90	Crème Brûlée	108
Gingerbread Cake	93	Chocolate Sheet Cake	110
Gingerbread Cake with Dried Fruit	94	Glazed Chocolate Bundt Cake	112
Prune-nut Bread	97	German Chocolate Cake	114
Lazy Daisy Cake	98	Warm Chocolate Fudge Cakes	117
Almond Meal Cake with Broiled Icing	100	Pineapple Cake	118
Italian Almond Cake	103	Lemon Pound Cake	121
Individual Bananas Foster Cakes	104	Carrot Cake	122
Chocolate Cupcakes	107		

Applesauce Snack Cake

SERVES 9

Ingredients

1 cup apple cider

¾ cup dried apples, cut into ½-inch pieces

1½ cups almond flour

1 teaspoon baking soda

⅔ cup palm sugar

½ teaspoon ground cinnamon

¼ teaspoon ground nutmeg

1/8 teaspoon ground cloves

½ teaspoon salt

1 cup unsweetened applesauce, room temperature

1 large egg, room temperature

8 tablespoons coconut oil, melted and cooled

1 teaspoon vanilla extract

Coconut oil for greasing foil

Preparation

1. Adjust oven rack to the middle position and preheat the oven to 325°F. Line an eight-inch square baking pan with a foil sling. Make a foil sling for an eight-inch square baking pan by folding two long sheets of aluminum foil so each is eight inches wide. Lay sheets of foil in pan perpendicular to each other, with extra foil hanging over edges of pan. Push foil into corners and up sides of pan, smoothing foil flush to pan. Grease the foil with coconut oil.

2. Simmer the cider and dried apples together in a small saucepan over medium heat until the liquid evaporates and the mixture looks dry (about 15 minutes). Let the mixture cool to room temperature.

3. Whisk flour and baking soda together in a medium bowl. In a smaller bowl, whisk the palm sugar, cinnamon, nutmeg, and cloves together; reserve two tablespoons of palm sugar-spice mixture for the topping.

4. Process the cooled apple mixture and applesauce together in a food processor until smooth (20 to 30 seconds).

5. In a large bowl, whisk the egg and salt together by hand. Whisk in the palm sugar-spice mixture until well combined and light-colored. Add the melted coconut oil, in three additions, whisking until combined. Whisk in the applesauce mixture and vanilla until combined. Lastly, fold in the flour mixture with a rubber spatula until just incorporated.

6. Scrape the batter into the prepared pan, smooth the top, and gently tap the pan on the counter to settle the batter. Sprinkle the reserved two tablespoons of palm sugar-spice mixture evenly over the top. Bake the cake until a toothpick inserted in center comes out with a few moist crumbs attached (35 to 40 minutes), rotating the pan halfway through baking.

7. Allow the cake to cool completely in the pan (one to two hours). If desired, remove the cake from the pan using the foil before serving.

Gingerbread Cake

SERVES 9

Ingredients

1¾ cups almond flour

2 teaspoons ground ginger

1 teaspoon cacao powder

1 teaspoon ground cinnamon

½ teaspoon ground cloves

½ teaspoon ground nutmeg

½ teaspoon ground allspice

½ teaspoon baking soda

½ teaspoon salt

¾ cup blackstrap molasses

¾ cup palm sugar

8 tablespoons coconut oil, melted and cooled

1 large egg, room temperature

1 cup coconut milk, room temperature

Preparation

1. Adjust oven rack to the middle position and preheat the oven to 325°F. Line an eight-inch square baking pan with a foil sling. Make a foil sling for an eight-inch square baking pan by folding two long sheets of aluminum foil so each is eight inches wide. Lay sheets of foil in pan perpendicular to each other, with extra foil hanging over edges of pan. Push foil into corners and up sides of pan, smoothing foil flush to pan. Grease the foil with coconut oil.

2. Whisk the flour, ginger, cacao powder, cinnamon, cloves, nutmeg, allspice, baking soda, and salt together in a medium bowl.

3. In a large bowl, beat the molasses, palm sugar, and melted coconut oil together with an electric mixer on low speed until combined (1 to 3 minutes). Beat in the egg until combined (about 30 seconds). Add the coconut milk and continue beating for about 30 seconds. Lastly, beat in the flour mixture until the batter is smooth and thick (1 to 3 minutes).

4. Scrape the batter into the prepared pan, smooth the top, and gently tap the pan on the counter to settle the batter. Bake the cake until a toothpick inserted in the center comes out with a few moist crumbs attached (35 to 40 minutes), rotating the pan halfway through baking.

5. Let the cake cool completely in the pan, one to two hours. If desired, remove the cake from the pan using the foil before serving.

Gingerbread Cake with Dried Fruit

SERVES 9

Ingredients

1¾ cups almond flour

2 teaspoons ground ginger

1 teaspoon cacao powder

1 teaspoon ground
   cinnamon

½ teaspoon ground cloves

½ teaspoon ground nutmeg

½ teaspoon ground allspice

½ teaspoon baking soda

½ teaspoon salt

¾ cup raisins, chopped
   prunes, or dried
   cranberries, unsweetened
   and additive free

¾ cup blackstrap molasses

¾ cup palm sugar

8 tablespoons coconut oil,
   melted and cooled

1 large egg, room
   temperature

¾ coconut milk, room
   temperature

Preparation

1. Adjust an oven rack to the middle position and preheat the oven to 350°F. Line an eight-inch square baking pan with a foil sling. Make a foil sling for an eight-inch square baking pan by folding two long sheets of aluminum foil so each is eight inches wide. Lay sheets of foil in pan perpendicular to each other, with extra foil hanging over edges of pan. Push foil into corners and up sides of pan, smoothing foil flush to pan. Grease the foil with coconut oil.

2. Whisk the flour, ginger, cacao powder, cinnamon, cloves, nutmeg, allspice, baking soda, and salt together in a medium bowl.

3. In a large bowl, beat the molasses, palm sugar, and melted coconut oil together with an electric mixer on low speed until combined. Beat in the egg until combined (about 30 seconds). Beat in the coconut milk until combined (about 30 seconds). Beat in the flour mixture until the batter is smooth and thick (1 to 3 minutes). Fold in the dried fruit (raisins, chopped prunes, or dried cranberries).

4. Scrape the batter into the prepared pan, smooth the top, and gently tap the pan on the counter to settle the batter. Bake the cake until a toothpick inserted in the center comes out with a few moist crumbs attached (35 to 40 minutes), rotating the pan halfway through baking.

5. Let the cake cool completely in the pan (one to two hours). If desired, remove the cake from the pan using the foil before serving.

Prune-Nut Bread

Ingredients

2 cups whole prunes, coarsely chopped

1 cup boiling water

1 teaspoon baking soda

2 cups almond flour

1 teaspoon baking powder

½ teaspoon salt

¾ cup palm sugar

⅔ cup coconut milk

1 teaspoon fresh lemon juice

6 tablespoons coconut oil, melted and cooled

1 large egg

1 cup pecans or walnuts, toasted and coarsely chopped

Preparation

1. Adjust an oven rack to the middle position and preheat the oven to 350°F. Grease a standard loaf pan.

2. Stir the prunes, water, and baking soda together in a medium bowl. Cover and set aside until the prunes have softened (about 30 minutes).

3. Whisk the flour, baking powder, and salt together in a large bowl. In a medium bowl, whisk the sugar, coconut milk, coconut oil, and egg together until smooth, then stir in the prune mixture until combined. Gently fold the coconut milk mixture into the flour mixture with a rubber spatula until just combined. Gently fold in nuts.

4. Scrape the batter into the prepared loaf pan and smooth the top. Bake until golden brown and a toothpick inserted into the center comes out with just a few crumbs attached (55 to 60 minutes), rotating the pan halfway through baking.

5. Let the loaf cool in the pan for 10 minutes, then turn out onto a wire rack and allow to cool for one hour before using in bread pudding or serving as is.

Lazy Daisy Cake

SERVES 9

Ingredients

Cake

1 cup almond flour

1 teaspoon baking powder

¼ teaspoon salt

½ cup coconut milk

2 tablespoons coconut oil

½ teaspoon vanilla extract

2 large eggs, room temperature

1 cup palm sugar

Coconut oil for greasing foil

Broiled Icing

½ cup honey

2 tablespoons coconut oil, melted and cooled

4 tablespoons coconut milk

1 cup unsweetened shredded coconut

Preparation

1. Adjust an oven rack to the middle position and preheat the oven to 350°F. Line an eight-inch square baking pan with a foil sling. Make a foil sling for an eight-inch square baking pan by folding two long sheets of aluminum foil so each is eight inches wide. Lay sheets of foil in pan perpendicular to each other, with extra foil hanging over edges of pan. Push foil into corners and up sides of pan, smoothing foil flush to pan. Grease foil.

2. Whisk the flour, baking powder, and salt together in a large bowl.

3. Heat the coconut milk, coconut oil, and vanilla together in a medium saucepan over medium heat until the coconut oil melts. Remove from heat and cover to keep warm.

4. In a large bowl, beat the eggs and palm sugar together with an electric mixer on medium-high speed until thick. Reduce the mixer speed to low and beat in one-third of the flour mixture, followed by half of the coconut milk mixture. Repeat with half of the remaining flour mixture, and then the remaining coconut milk mixture. Lastly, beat in the remaining flour mixture until just incorporated.

5. Scrape the batter into the prepared pan, smooth the top, and gently tap the pan on the counter to settle the batter. Bake the cake until a toothpick inserted in the center comes out with a few moist crumbs attached (30 to 35 minutes), rotating the pan halfway through baking. Cool slightly in the pan for about 10 minutes.
6. While the cake is cooling, adjust the oven rack to be about nine inches from the broiler element and heat the broiler. In a medium bowl, whisk the honey, melted coconut oil, and coconut milk together, then stir in the coconut. Spread the mixture evenly over the still-warm cake and broil until the topping is bubbling and golden (3 to 5 minutes), checking often to ensure the icing is not burning.
7. Let the cake cool slightly in the pan (about 30 minutes). If desired, remove the cake from the pan using the foil before serving.

Almond Meal Cake With Broiled Icing

SERVES 9

Ingredients

Cake

1 cup almond meal

¾ cup water, room temperature

¾ cup almond flour

½ teaspoon baking soda

½ teaspoon baking powder

½ teaspoon salt

¼ teaspoon ground cinnamon

⅛ teaspoon ground nutmeg

4 tablespoons coconut oil, softened

1 cup palm sugar, divided

1 large egg, room temperature

½ teaspoon vanilla extract

Coconut oil for greasing foil

Broiled Icing

¼ cup honey

1 tablespoon coconut oil, melted and cooled

2 tablespoons coconut milk

¾ cup unsweetened shredded coconut

½ cup pecans, chopped

Preparation

1. Adjust an oven rack to the middle position and preheat the oven to 350°F. Line an eight-inch square baking pan with a foil sling. Make a foil sling for an eight-inch square baking pan by folding two long sheets of aluminum foil so each is eight inches wide. Lay sheets of foil in pan perpendicular to each other, with extra foil hanging over edges of pan. Push foil into corners and up sides of pan, smoothing foil flush to pan. Grease the foil.

2. Combine almond meal and water in a medium bowl and let sit until most of the water is absorbed (about 10 minutes). In another medium bowl, whisk the flour, baking soda, baking powder, salt, cinnamon, and nutmeg together.

3. In a large bowl, beat the coconut oil and palm sugar together with an electric mixer on medium speed until light and fluffy. Beat in the egg and vanilla until combined (about 30 seconds). Beat in the flour mixture, in two additions, until just incorporated (about 30 seconds). Beat in the soaked almond meal until

combined. Use a spatula to transfer the batter from the mixing bowl into the baking pan.

4. Bake the cake until a toothpick inserted in the center comes out with a few moist crumbs attached (30 to 35 minutes), rotating the pan halfway through baking. Let the cake cool slightly in the pan (about 10 minutes).

5. While the cake is cooling, adjust an oven rack to be about nine inches from the broiler element and heat the broiler. In a medium bowl whisk the honey, melted coconut oil, and coconut milk together, then stir in the coconut and pecans. Spread the mixture evenly over the warm cake and broil until the topping is bubbling and golden (3 to 5 minutes), checking often to ensure that the icing is not burning.

6. Let the cake cool slightly in the pan (about 30 minutes). If desired, remove the cake from the pan using the foil before serving.

Italian Almond Cake

SERVES 8 TO 10

Ingredients

2½ cups slivered almonds, toasted
1 cup palm sugar
1 pinch salt
½ cup coconut flour
½ teaspoon baking powder

6 tablespoons coconut oil, cut into 6 pieces
  and softened
4 large eggs, room temperature
⅓ cup whole coconut milk
1 Fruit Jam recipe (page 221)

Preparation

1. Adjust an oven rack to the middle position and preheat the oven to 350°F. Grease a nine-inch round cake pan, then line the bottom with parchment paper.
2. Process the almonds, ¼ cup of the palm sugar, and the salt together in a food processor until very finely ground (about 15 seconds). Add the flour and baking powder and pulse to incorporate (about 5 pulses).
3. Beat the coconut oil and remaining ¾ cup palm sugar together in a large bowl with an electric mixer on medium speed until light and fluffy (3 to 6 minutes). Beat in the eggs one at a time until combined (about 30 seconds). Reduce the mixer speed to low and beat in the ground almond mixture until incorporated (about 30 seconds). Beat in the coconut milk until combined (about 20 seconds).
4. Give the batter a final stir with a rubber spatula to make sure it is thoroughly combined. Scrape the batter into the prepared pan, smooth the top, and gently tap the pan on the counter to settle the batter. Bake the cake until the top is golden and a toothpick inserted in the center comes out clean (25 to 30 minutes), rotating the pan halfway through baking.
5. Let the cake cool in the pan for 10 minutes. Run a small knife around the edge of the cake, then flip it out onto a wire rack. Peel off the parchment paper, flip the cake right side up, and allow to cool for about two hours. The cake can be served warm or at room temperature.

Making the Cake Ahead

The cooled cake can be wrapped in plastic wrap and refrigerated for up to 24 hours or wrapped in plastic wrap and foil and frozen for up to one month. If frozen, thaw the cake completely at room temperature (do not unwrap), for about four hours. Before serving, heat the cake at 350°F for 5 minutes to refresh, or for 10 to 15 minutes to warm.

Individual Bananas Foster Cakes

SERVES 8

Ingredients

14 tablespoons coconut oil (use 1 tablespoon of the oil for greasing the ramekins)

4 tablespoons honey

¼ cup dark rum or ½ teaspoon rum extract

3 medium bananas, peeled and sliced ¼-inch thick

½ cup coconut milk

2 large eggs, room temperature

2 teaspoons vanilla extract

1¾ cups almond flour

¾ cup palm sugar

2 teaspoons baking powder

¾ teaspoon salt

¾ teaspoon ground cinnamon

½ teaspoon lemon zest, fresh grated

Preparation

1. Adjust an oven rack to the middle position and preheat the oven to 325°F. Grease eight six-ounce ramekins, then set them on a large rimmed baking sheet.
2. Whisk the rum, coconut milk, eggs, and vanilla together in a medium bowl. Set aside.
3. In a large bowl, whisk the palm sugar, flour, baking powder, salt, cinnamon, and lemon zest together. Using an electric mixer on medium-low speed, beat the remaining coconut oil into the flour mixture and continue to beat the mixture until it resembles moist crumbs.
4. Beat in the coconut milk mixture (from step 2), then increase the mixer speed to medium and beat the batter until smooth, light, and fluffy.
5. Give the batter a final stir with a rubber spatula to make sure it is thoroughly combined. Spoon the batter evenly into the prepared ramekins, smooth the tops, and gently tap the ramekins on the counter to settle the batter. Shingle the banana slices on top of the batter inside each ramekin. Bake the cakes on the rimmed baking sheet until a toothpick inserted into the center comes out with a few crumbs attached (25 to 30 minutes), rotating the baking sheet halfway through the baking.

6. Immediately run a small knife around the edge of the cakes, gently invert each ramekin onto an individual serving plate, and let sit until the cakes release themselves from the ramekins (about 5 minutes). Remove the ramekins and serve.

Making the Cakes Ahead

After portioning the batter into the ramekins, wrap the ramekins tightly in plastic wrap and refrigerate for up to 24 hours. Let the ramekins sit at room temperature for 30 minutes, then bake as directed.

Chocolate Cupcakes

SERVES 12

Ingredients

2 ounces cacao nibs, chopped fine

⅓ cup cacao powder

¾ teaspoon instant espresso powder

¾ cup boiling water

¾ cup coconut flour

¾ cup palm sugar

½ teaspoon salt

½ teaspoon baking soda

5 tablespoons coconut oil

2 large eggs

1 teaspoon vanilla extract

2 cups chocolate frosting
  (recipe follows)

4 tablespoons coconut oil

4 tablespoons coconut milk

8 tablespoons cacao nibs

4 teaspoons cacao powder

Preparation

1. Adjust oven rack to middle position and preheat oven to 350°F. Line a twelve-cup muffin tin with paper or foil liners.

2. Combine cacao nibs, cacao powder, and espresso powder in large bowl. Pour boiling water over top, cover, and let sit for 5 minutes to melt cacao nibs. Whisk the mixture until smooth, then set it aside to cool slightly. In a separate bowl, whisk flour, palm sugar, salt, and baking soda together.

3. Whisk oil, eggs, and vanilla into the cooled cacao nibs mixture until smooth. Whisk in flour mixture, also until smooth. Using a greased quarter-cup measure, portion batter into prepared muffin cups.

4. Bake cupcakes until a toothpick inserted in the center comes out with few moist crumbs attached (17 to 19 minutes), rotating pan halfway through baking. Let cupcakes cool in the pan on wire rack for 10 minutes. Remove cupcakes from pan and allow to cool completely on rack for about one hour. Using a small icing spatula, frost each cupcake with about 2½ tablespoons frosting. Serve.

Chocolate Frosting

Mix all frosting ingredients and microwave until coconut oil melts (30 to 45 seconds). Whisk and refrigerate until thickened.

Crème Brûlée

SERVES 8

Ingredients

2 ounces dairy-free white chocolate, chopped

1 vanilla bean, cut in half lengthwise, seeds scraped out and reserved

3½ cups coconut milk

⅓ cup palm sugar

¼ teaspoon salt

5 large egg yolks

3 tablespoons tapioca flour

8 teaspoons palm sugar

Preparation

1. Adjust oven rack to middle position and preheat oven to 300°F.
2. Place white chocolate in an eight-cup liquid measuring cup.
3. Combine vanilla bean, seeds, coconut milk, palm sugar, and salt in a large saucepan. Whisk egg yolks and tapioca flour together in a bowl until combined, then whisk into saucepan. Bring to boil over medium heat, stirring constantly, then reduce heat to medium-low; simmer until thickened, about one minute.
4. Strain boiled mixture through a fine-mesh strainer into the liquid measuring cup with the white chocolate; whisk together until chocolate is melted and custard is completely smooth.
5. Bring two quarts of water to a boil. Place a kitchen towel in the bottom of a roasting pan. Arrange eight four- to five-ounce ramekins (or fluted dishes) on towel. Divide custard mixture evenly among ramekins. Carefully place pan on oven rack and pour boiling water into pan until water comes halfway up the sides of the ramekins. Bake until custard is just set and center registers 170°F, or about 30 minutes (about 20 minutes if using shallow fluted dishes).
6. Carefully transfer ramekins to a wire rack and cool to room temperature (about two hours). Cover with plastic wrap and refrigerate until well chilled and set (at least four hours, or up to two days).
7. Gently blot away any condensation using paper towels. Sprinkle 1 teaspoon palm sugar evenly over each custard. Caramelize palm sugar with a torch until it turns a deep golden brown. Serve.

Chocolate Sheet Cake

SERVES 16

Ingredients

3 ounces cacao nibs, chopped

1 tablespoon coconut oil

1 tablespoon palm sugar

½ tablespoon cacao powder

1½ cups almond flour

¾ cup cacao powder

1 teaspoon baking powder

1 teaspoon baking soda

¼ teaspoon salt

6 tablespoons coconut oil

1¼ cups palm sugar

4 large eggs

1 teaspoon vanilla extract

2 teaspoons instant espresso powder

1½ cups coconut milk

Chocolate Frosting

4 tablespoons coconut oil

4 tablespoons coconut milk

8 tablespoons cacao nibs

4 teaspoons cacao powder

Coconut oil for greasing pan

Preparation

1. Adjust oven rack to middle position and preheat oven to 350°F. Grease a 13x9 baking pan with coconut oil and line the bottom with parchment paper.

2. Microwave cacao nibs, 1 tablespoon coconut oil, and 1 tablespoon palm sugar in a covered bowl, stirring occasionally, until melted and smooth (1 to 3 minutes). Allow to cool slightly.

3. In a separate bowl, whisk flour, cacao powder, baking powder, baking soda, and salt together.

4. In a medium bowl, add 6 tablespoons of coconut oil and 1¼ cups palm sugar and combine with a whisk. Add melted cacao nibs mixture and whisk until the mixture looks thick and grainy. Add eggs, vanilla, and espresso powder and whisk to combine. Add flour mixture in three additions, alternating with two additions of coconut milk, stirring with a sturdy spoon and scraping down bowl as needed. Give batter final stir by hand.

5. Pour batter into prepared pan and smooth top. Bake until a toothpick inserted in center comes out with few moist crumbs attached (25 to 30 minutes). Allow the cake to cool completely in the pan on a wire rack (about one-and-a-half hours). Spread frosting over top of cake and cut into sixteen pieces. Serve.

Chocolate Frosting

Mix all frosting ingredients and microwave until coconut oil melts (30 to 45 seconds). Whisk and refrigerate until thickened.

Glazed Chocolate Bundt Cake

Serves 16

Ingredients

Cake

3 ounces cacao nibs, chopped fine

¾ cup cacao powder

1 teaspoon instant espresso powder

1 cup boiling water

1¾ cups almond flour

1 teaspoon baking soda

1 teaspoon salt

2 cups palm sugar

½ cup coconut oil

4 large eggs, room temperature

1 tablespoon vanilla extract

Coconut oil for greasing Bundt pan

Vanilla Glaze (optional)

1 cup palm sugar

1 tablespoon coconut milk

1 tablespoon vanilla extract

1 pinch salt

Preparation

1. Adjust oven rack to a lower-middle position and preheat oven to 350°F. Grease the inside of a twelve-cup Bundt pan thoroughly with coconut oil.
2. Combine cacao nibs, cacao powder, and instant espresso powder in a large bowl. Pour the cup of boiling water over top and cover. Let sit for 5 minutes to melt the cacao nibs, then whisk smooth.
3. In a separate bowl, whisk flour, baking soda, and salt together.
4. Process melted cacao nibs mixture, palm sugar, oil, eggs, and vanilla together in food processor until combined (about 1 minute). Transfer to a large bowl. Sift one-third of the flour mixture over batter and whisk until just a few streaks of flour remain. Repeat twice more with remaining flour mixture, then continue to whisk batter gently until most lumps are gone (do not overmix).
5. Scrape batter into prepared pan and smooth top. Wipe any drops of batter off sides of pan and gently tap pan on counter to settle batter. Bake until a toothpick inserted in center comes out clean (50 to 60 minutes), rotating pan halfway through baking. Allow cake to cool in the pan on a wire rack for 10 minutes. Remove cake from pan and cool completely on rack for about two hours.

For the Vanilla Glaze

Whisk all glaze ingredients together in a bowl until smooth, then drizzle evenly over the top of the cooled cake, letting it drip down the sides. Let glaze set for 15 minutes before serving.

German Chocolate Cake

SERVES 12

Ingredients

Cake

3 ounces cacao nibs, chopped

3 tablespoons cacao powder

⅓ cup boiling water

1⅓ cups almond flour

½ teaspoon baking soda

3 tablespoons coconut oil, softened

⅚ cup palm sugar

½ teaspoon salt

6 large eggs, room temperature

1 teaspoon vanilla extract

½ cup coconut milk

Frosting

1⅓ cup palm sugar

2 cups coconut milk

6 tablespoons tapioca flour

4 tablespoons coconut oil

½ teaspoon salt

2 tablespoons vanilla extract

1 shredded coconut, toasted

⅔ cup pecans, toasted and chopped fine

Preparation

1. Adjust oven rack to a lower-middle position and preheat oven to 350°F. Grease two nine-inch round cake pans, line with parchment paper. Grease parchment, then flour pans.

2. Combine cacao nibs and cacao powder together in a medium bowl, pour boiling water over top, and cover. Let sit for 5 minutes to melt cacao nibs, then whisk smooth.

3. In a separate bowl, whisk flour and baking soda together.

4. Using a stand mixer fitted with paddle, beat coconut oil, palm sugar, and salt on medium-high speed for about 30 seconds or until well combined. Add eggs, one at a time, and beat until combined. Reduce speed to low and add cacao nibs mixture and vanilla, beating until incorporated. Add flour mixture in three additions, alternating with two additions of coconut milk, scraping down bowl as needed. Give batter a final stir by hand.

5. Divide batter evenly between pans. Bake until a toothpick inserted in center comes out clean (10 to 15 minutes). Let cool in pans on wire rack for 10 minutes.

Remove cakes from pans, discard parchment, and let cool completely on rack (about two hours).

6. Combine palm sugar, coconut milk, tapioca flour, coconut oil, and salt together in a small saucepan. Bring to a simmer over medium-high heat and cook, whisking constantly, until just thickened (about 1 to 3 minutes). Remove from heat and stir in vanilla and all but one tablespoon each of the coconut and pecans. Allow to cool to room temperature. Pour off any oil that has separated before mixing and frosting the cake.

7. Cover the edges of a cake platter with strips of parchment. Place one cake layer on the platter. Spread half of the frosting evenly over top, right to the edge of the cake. Top with sthe econd cake layer, pressing lightly to adhere, then spread remaining frosting evenly over top of cake, leaving sides unfrosted. Sprinkle with remaining coconut and pecans. Carefully remove parchment strips before serving.

Warm Chocolate Fudge Cakes

SERVES 8

Ingredients

1½ cups almond flour

1 cup cacao powder

1 teaspoon baking powder

½ teaspoon baking soda

½ teaspoon salt

1¼ cups coconut milk

1½ cups palm sugar

¼ cup coconut oil

4 large eggs

1 teaspoon vanilla extract

2 ounces baking cacao, divided into 8 equal pieces

Coconut oil for greasing ramekins

Preparation

1. Adjust oven rack to middle position and preheat oven to 350°F. Grease and flour eight six-ounce ramekins and arrange on a rimmed baking sheet.

2. Whisk flour, cacao powder, baking powder, baking soda, and salt together in a bowl. In another large bowl, whisk coconut milk, palm sugar, oil, eggs, and vanilla together. Slowly whisk flour mixture into coconut milk mixture until combined.

3. Press batter into prepared ramekins, dividing equally. (Batter will be thick, like cookie dough.) Gently press a piece of cacao into the center of each ramekin to submerge. Bake until cakes rise and the tops turn glossy (about 20 minutes, rotating sheet halfway through baking); the center should be gooey when pierced with a skewer. Do not overbake. Serve warm.

Pineapple Cake

SERVES 16-24

Ingredients

Pineapple Topping

4 cups frozen pineapple, thawed and cut
    into ½-inch pieces

⅓ cup palm sugar

1½ tablespoons coconut oil

2 teaspoons lemon juice

½ teaspoon vanilla extract

Coconut oil for greasing cake pan

Cake

1 cup almond flour

1 teaspoon baking powder

½ teaspoon salt

½ cup coconut milk

¾ palm sugar

2 large eggs

1½ teaspoons vanilla extract

4 tablespoons coconut oil, melted and
    cooled

Preparation

1. Adjust oven rack to middle position and preheat oven to 350°F. Grease a 9x13 cake pan.

2. Cook pineapple and palm sugar in a twelve-inch skillet over medium-high heat, stirring often, until pineapple is light brown and juices are nearly evaporated (12 to 15 minutes). Remove from heat and stir in coconut oil, lemon juice, and vanilla. Transfer pineapple mixture to prepared pan and smooth into an even layer.

3. Whisk flour, baking powder, and salt together in a medium bowl. In a separate large bowl, whisk sour cream, palm sugar, eggs, and vanilla together until smooth. Slowly whisk in melted coconut oil until incorporated. Lastly, whisk in flour mixture until just incorporated (do not overmix).

4. Scrape batter evenly into pan, covering pineapple completely. Bake until cake is golden and a toothpick inserted into the center comes out clean (25 to 30 minutes), rotating pan halfway through baking. Allow the cake to cool in the pan on a wire rack for 10 minutes. Turn cake out onto platter and let cool for at least one hour before serving.

Lemon Pound Cake

Ingredients

Cake

1½ cups almond flour

½ teaspoon baking powder

¼ teaspoon salt

⅓ cup coconut milk

½ teaspoon tapioca flour

1½ tablespoons grated lemon zest plus

1½ tablespoons lemon juice

½ teaspoon vanilla extract

1 cup palm sugar

6 tablespoons coconut oil

3 large eggs, room temperature

Coconut oil for greasing loaf pan

Glaze

⅓ cup honey

1 tablespoon lemon juice

Preparation

1. Adjust oven rack to middle position and preheat oven to 300°F. Grease an 8x4 loaf pan.

2. Whisk almond flour, baking powder, and salt together in bowl. In a separate bowl, whisk coconut milk, lemon juice, and vanilla together. In a third bowl, whisk palm sugar and lemon zest together until well combined.

3. Using a stand mixer fitted with a paddle, beat coconut oil and palm sugar-zest mixture on medium-high speed for about 1 minute. Add eggs, one at a time, and mix until combined (batter may look slightly curdled). Reduce speed to low and add almond flour mixture in three additions, alternating with coconut milk mixture in two additions, scraping down bowl as needed. Give batter a final stir by hand.

4. Scrape batter into prepared pan and smooth top. Gently tap pan on counter to release air bubbles. Bake until the cake is golden brown and a toothpick inserted in the center comes out with a few moist crumbs attached (60 to 70 minutes), rotating pan halfway through baking. Allow cake to cool in the pan on a wire rack for 10 minutes. Remove cake from pan and let cool completely (about two hours).

5. Whisk honey and lemon juice together in a bowl until smooth. Brush glaze over cake and let sit for 10 minutes before serving.

Carrot Cake

SERVES 16-24

Ingredients

2½ cups almond flour

2 teaspoons baking powder

1 teaspoon baking soda

1½ teaspoons ground cinnamon

½ teaspoon ground nutmeg

½ teaspoon salt

⅛ teaspoon ground cloves

4 large eggs

2 cups palm sugar

½ cup coconut oil

1 pound carrots, peeled and grated

Coconut oil for greasing pan

Preparation

1. Adjust oven rack to middle position and preheat oven to 350°F. Grease a 13x9 baking pan, then line bottom of pan with parchment paper.

2. Whisk flour, baking powder, baking soda, cinnamon, nutmeg, salt, and cloves together in a bowl.

3. In a large bowl, whisk eggs and palm sugar until the sugar is mostly dissolved and the mixture is frothy. Continue to whisk and slowly add oil, mixing until thoroughly incorporated and emulsified. Whisk flour mixture in two additions, scraping down bowl as needed, until just incorporated. Stir in carrots.

4. Scrape batter into prepared pan and smooth top. Gently tap pan on counter to release air bubbles. Bake cake until a toothpick inserted in the center comes out with a few moist crumbs attached (35 to 40 minutes), rotating pan halfway through baking.

5. Allow the cake to cool completely in the pan on a wire rack (about two hours). Run a paring knife around the edge of the cake and flip the cake out onto a wire rack. Peel off the parchment paper. Then flip the cake right side up onto a serving platter. Serve warm or at room temperature.

{ Pies }

Chocolate Cream Pie   126

Key Lime Pie   129

Almond Butter Pie   130

Chocolate Cream Pie

Serves 8

Ingredients

Crust

4½ ounces almond flour

3 tablespoons palm sugar, plus 1 additional tablespoon palm sugar

3 tablespoons coconut oil, melted

2 ounces coconut milk

2 teaspoons coconut oil

Coconut oil for greasing pie plate

Pie

1 cup palm sugar

6 tablespoons tapioca flour

4 tablespoons cacao powder

¼ teaspoon salt

5 cups coconut milk

2 large eggs, lightly beaten

8 ounces cacao nibs, finely chopped

5 teaspoons vanilla extract

1 cup coconut milk

2 tablespoons palm sugar

3 large egg whites

¼ teaspoon lemon juice

1 teaspoon tapioca flour

Preparation

1. Adjust oven rack to middle position and preheat oven to 350°F. Grease a nine-inch pie plate with coconut oil.

2. Process almond flour and one tablespoon of palm sugar into fine crumbs in a food processor (about 10 seconds). Add coconut oil and coconut milk and pulse until combined (about 8 pulses). Press crumbs into bottom and up sides of prepared pie plate.

3. Bake crust until top edge is slightly lighter in color and crust is set (about 15 minutes). Allow to cool completely (about 30 minutes).

4. Combine palm sugar, tapioca flour, cacao powder, and salt in a bowl.

5. Whisk coconut milk and eggs together in a medium saucepan, then whisk in palm sugar mixture. Add cacao nibs and bring to a boil over medium heat, whisking constantly. Reduce heat to low and cook, whisking constantly, until

mixture becomes thick and glossy (about 3 minutes). Remove from heat and stir in two teaspoons of vanilla.

6. Strain mixture through a fine-mesh strainer into the cooled crust. Place plastic wrap directly on the surface of the pudding to prevent a skin from forming. Refrigerate until completely cool (at least three hours, or up to one day).

7. Using a stand mixer fitted with a whisk, whip egg whites, lemon juice, tapioca flour, coconut milk, and palm sugar until foamy (about 1 minute). Increase speed to high and whip until soft peaks form (2 to 3 minutes). Spread whipped topping evenly over pie and cut pie into eight slices. Serve.

Key Lime Pie

SERVES 8

Ingredients

2¼ cups almond flour

1 tablespoon palm sugar

3 tablespoons coconut oil, melted and cooled

½ cup coconut milk

¾ tablespoon tapioca flour

1¼ teaspoons tapioca flour

1 tablespoon grated lime zest

¾ cup lime juice (6 limes)

6 ounces coconut milk

8 ounces honey

½ cup coconut milk

1 teaspoon vanilla extract

Coconut oil for greasing pie plate

Preparation

1. Adjust oven rack to middle position and preheat oven to 325°F. Lightly grease a nine-inch pie plate with coconut oil.
2. Process almond flour and palm sugar together into fine, even crumbs in a food processor (about 30 seconds). Add 3 tablespoons melted and cooled coconut oil to the food processor and pulse to incorporate (about 5 pulses).
3. Sprinkle mixture into prepared pie plate. Using the bottom of a measuring cup, press crumbs into an even layer on the bottom and sides of the pie plate. Bake crust until fragrant and beginning to brown (12 to 14 minutes). Allow to cool completely on a wire rack (about 45 minutes).
4. Add ½ cup coconut milk and ¾ tablespoon tapioca flour to a bowl and whisk until smooth. Let stand for 5 minutes.
5. Sprinkle 1¼ tablespoons of tapioca flour over three tablespoons lime juice in a bowl and whisk together. Microwave until mixture is bubbling around the edges and tapioca flour dissolves (about 30 seconds). Whisk again and set aside.
6. Whisk together 6 ounces of coconut milk and 8 ounces of honey in a bowl. Set aside.
7. Process coconut milk and tapioca flour mixture together in a food processor, then add the coconut milk and honey mixture and continue processing until smooth (about 1 minute). With processor still running, add the remaining 6 ounces of coconut milk, nine tablespoons of lime juice, lime zest, and vanilla. Process until thoroughly combined (about 1 minute). Add the entire contents of the food processor to a saucepan and heat over medium-high heat, whisking constantly, until thickened (5 to 7 minutes). Cool to room temperature.
8. Scrape mixture into the cooled pie shell and smooth top. Cover with plastic wrap and refrigerate until firm (at least three hours, or up to two days). Cut pie into eight slices and serve.

Almond Butter Pie

Ingredients

Crust

2 cups almond flour

¼ cup cacao powder

¼ cup palm sugar

5 teaspoons water

3 tablespoons coconut oil, melted and cooled

2 tablespoons coconut milk

Filling

¾ cup marshmallows (see Paleo Marshmallow recipe, page 87)

2 cups almond butter

1 teaspoon vanilla extract

¼ teaspoon salt

½ cup coconut milk, warmed

Preparation

1. Adjust the oven rack to the middle position and preheat oven to 350°F.

2. Process almond flour, cacao powder, and palm sugar in a food processor until finely ground (about 15 seconds). Add coconut oil and coconut milk and pulse to incorporate (about 5 pulses).

3. Press mixture into nine-inch pie plate greased with coconut oil. Using the bottom of a measuring cup, press crumbs into an even layer on the bottom and sides of the plate. Bake until crust is fragrant and looks slightly dried out (about 30 minutes). Allow to cool completely on a wire rack (about 45 minutes).

4. Place marshmallows in a microwave safe bowl and microwave until just beginning to melt, 10–30 seconds. Using a stand mixer fitted with a whisk, mix melted marshmallows, almond butter, coconut milk, vanilla, and salt on medium speed until combined and smooth (about 1 minute). Reduce speed to medium-low until incorporated and no streaks remain (1 to 2 minutes).

5. Scrape mixture into the cooled pie shell and smooth top. Cover with plastic wrap and refrigerate until filling is chilled and set (at least eight hours, or up to one day). Cut pie into eight slices and serve.

{ Tarts }

Classic Tart Dough   135

Strawberry Tart   136

Poached Apple and Almond Tart   138

Poached Pear and Almond Tart   140

Baked Raspberry Tart   144

Cranberry Pecan Tart   146

Linzertorte   149

Lemon Tart   152

Chocolate Truffle Tart   155

Chocolate Walnut Tart   156

Espresso Truffle Tart   160

Classic Tart Dough

Ingredients

2 large eggs
1 tablespoon coconut milk
½ teaspoon vanilla
¾ cup coconut flour
½ cup almond flour
⅔ cup palm sugar
¼ teaspoon salt
8 tablespoons coconut oil

Preparation

1. Whisk the egg, coconut milk, and vanilla together in a small bowl.
2. In a separate bowl, whisk the flours, sugar, and salt together until combined. Add the coconut oil to the flour mixture and mix until it resembles coarse cornmeal.
3. While continuing to whisk, add the egg mixture and stir until dough just comes together.
4. Turn the dough onto a sheet of plastic wrap and flatten into a six-inch disk. Wrap the dough tightly in the plastic wrap and refrigerate for one hour. Before rolling the dough out, let it sit on the counter to soften slightly (about 10 minutes).

Strawberry Tart

Ingredients

1 recipe Classic Tart Dough (page 135)

Pastry Cream

2 cups coconut milk

½ cup palm sugar

1 pinch salt

½ vanilla bean, halved lengthwise, seeds
  removed and reserved

5 large egg yolks

3 tablespoons tapioca flour

4 tablespoons coconut oil, cut into ½-inch
  pieces and chilled

Fruit

3 quarts strawberries, hulled and sorted by
  height

½ cup strawberry jam (See Fruit Jam
  recipe)

Preparation

1. Bring the coconut milk, 6 tablespoons of the palm sugar, salt, vanilla bean, and vanilla seeds to a simmer in a medium saucepan over medium-high heat, stirring occasionally.

2. As the coconut milk mixture begins to simmer, whisk the egg yolks, tapioca flour, and remaining two tablespoons palm sugar together in a medium bowl until smooth. Slowly whisk about 1 cup of the simmering coconut mixture into the yolks to temper, and then slowly whisk the tempered yolks back into the simmering saucepan. Reduce the heat to medium and cook, whisking vigorously, until the mixture is thickened and a few bubbles burst on the surface (about 30 seconds).

3. Remove from heat. Discard the vanilla bean and stir the coconut oil into the mixture. Transfer to a medium bowl, lay a sheet of plastic wrap directly on the surface, and refrigerate the pastry cream until chilled and firm (about three hours).

4. Roll the tart dough out to an eleven-inch circle on a lightly floured counter and fit into a nine-inch tart pan with a removable bottom, or press into individual fluted mini-tart cups. Set the tart pan or mini-tart cups on a large plate and freeze the tart shell for 30 minutes.

5. Adjust an oven rack to the middle position and preheat the oven to 375°F. Set the tart pan or mini-tart cups on a large baking sheet. Bake until the tart shell is golden brown and set (about 30 minutes for full-size tart, or 10 to 15 minutes for mini-tarts), rotating the baking sheet halfway through baking.
6. Transfer the baking sheet to a wire rack and allow the tart shell to cool completely on the baking sheet (about one hour).
7. Spread the chilled pastry cream evenly over the bottom of the cooled tart shell. Starting in the center with the largest strawberries, arrange the fruit in tight, concentric circles over the tart. Quarter the remaining strawberries and use them to fill gaps, or cut thirteen individual strawberries into fan shapes and place one on each mini-tart.
8. Melt the fruit jam in a small saucepan over medium-high heat, stirring occasionally to smooth out any lumps. Using a pastry brush, dab the melted fruit jam over the fruit. To serve, remove the outer metal ring of the tart pan, slide a thin metal spatula between the tart and pan bottom, and carefully slide the tart onto a serving platter or cutting board. For mini-tarts, gently remove them from their cups and place on a serving platter.

Poached Apple Tart

MAKES ONE NINE-INCH TART OR THIRTEEN FLUTED MINI-TART CUPS

Ingredients

1 recipe Classic Tart Dough (page 135)

Poached Apples

3 cups apple cider

⅔ cup palm sugar

4 strips fresh lemon zest

2 tablespoons fresh lemon juice

1 cinnamon stick

½ vanilla bean, halved lengthwise with seeds removed and reserved, or 1 teaspoon vanilla extract

½ teaspoon whole black peppercorns

3 whole cloves

⅛ teaspoon salt

3 apples, halved lengthwise and cored

Filling and Glaze

¾ cup blanched, slivered almonds

⅓ cup palm sugar

⅛ teaspoon salt

1 large egg

½ teaspoon almond extract

½ teaspoon vanilla extract

4 tablespoons coconut oil, cut into 4 pieces

¼ cup fruit jam (see Fruit Jam recipe)

Preparation

1. Roll the dough out to an eleven-inch circle on a lightly floured counter and fit into a nine-inch tart pan with a removable bottom, or press dough evenly into thirteen fluted mini-tart cups. Set the tart pan or mini-tart cups on a large plate and freeze the tart shell for 30 minutes.

2. Adjust an oven rack to the middle position and preheat the oven to 375°F. Set the tart pan or mini-tart cups on a large baking sheet. Bake until the tart shell is golden brown and set (about 30 minutes for full-size tart, or 10 to 15 minutes for mini-tarts), rotating the baking sheet halfway through baking. Transfer the baking sheet to a wire rack and let the tart shell or mini-tart shells cool completely on the baking sheet (about one hour). While the crust is cooling, bring the apple cider, palm sugar, lemon zest, lemon

juice, cinnamon stick, vanilla bean, vanilla seeds, peppercorns, cloves, and salt to a boil in a medium saucepan, stirring to dissolve the palm sugar (about 5 minutes). Add the apples and return to a brief simmer, then reduce the heat to low, cover, and poach the apples, turning them occasionally, until tender and a skewer can be inserted into each apple with little resistance (10 to 20 minutes). Remove the pot from the heat and let the apples cool in the poaching liquid (about one hour).

3. Preheat the oven again to 350°F.

4. Pulse the almonds, palm sugar, and salt together in a food processor until finely ground (about 1 minute). Add the egg and extracts and process until combined (about 10 seconds). Add the coconut oil and process until no lumps remain (about 30 seconds). Spread the mixture evenly into the cooled tart shell, or spoon evenly into mini-tart cups.

5. Remove the cooled apples from the poaching liquid and pat them dry thoroughly with paper towels. Slice and arrange the apple halves over the tart (quarter of an apple, sliced, per two mini-tarts). Bake the tart(s) on the baking sheet until the almond filling is puffed, browned, and firm to the touch (about 45 minutes for the full-size tart and 15 to 20 minutes for the mini-tarts), rotating the baking sheet halfway through baking. Transfer the baking sheet to a wire rack to cool.

6. Melt the fruit jam in a small saucepan over medium-high heat, stirring occasionally to smooth out any lumps. Using a pastry brush, dab the melted fruit jam over the fruit. To serve, remove the outer metal ring of the tart pan, slide a thin metal spatula between the tart and pan bottom, and carefully slide the tart onto a serving platter or cutting board. For mini-tarts, gently remove them from their cups and place on a serving platter.

Making the Tart(s) Ahead

The tart dough can be made ahead, as instructed in the original recipe. The poached apples, submerged in the poaching liquid, can be refrigerated in an airtight container for up to three days. The almond filling can also be refrigerated in an airtight container for up to three days. Once baked, the tart can be wrapped loosely with plastic wrap and held at room temperature for up to four hours before serving.

Poached Pear and Almond Tart

MAKES ONE NINE-INCH TART OR THIRTEEN FLUTED MINI-TART CUPS

Ingredients

1 recipe Classic Tart Dough (page 135)

Poached Pears
3 cups apple cider

⅔ cup palm sugar

4 strips fresh lemon zest

2 tablespoons fresh lemon juice

1 cinnamon stick

½ vanilla bean, halved lengthwise with seeds removed and reserved, or 1 teaspoon vanilla extract

½ teaspoon whole black peppercorns

3 whole cloves

⅛ teaspoon salt

3 Bosc or Bartlett pears peeled, halved lengthwise, and cored

Filling and Glaze
¾ cup blanched, slivered almonds

⅓ cup palm sugar

⅛ teaspoon salt

1 large egg

½ teaspoon almond extract

½ teaspoon vanilla extract

4 tablespoons coconut oil, cut into 4 pieces

¼ cup fruit jam (see Fruit Jam recipe)

Preparation

1. Roll the dough out to an eleven-inch circle on a lightly floured counter and fit into a nine-inch tart pan with a removable bottom, or press dough evenly into

thirteen fluted mini-tart cups. Set the tart pan or mini-tart cups on a large plate and freeze the tart shell for 30 minutes.

2. Adjust an oven rack to the middle position and preheat the oven to 375°F. Set the tart pan or mini-tart cups on a large baking sheet. Bake until the tart shell is golden brown and set (about 30 minutes for full-size tart, or 10 to 15 minutes for mini-tarts), rotating the baking sheet halfway through baking. Transfer the baking sheet to a wire rack and let the tart shell or mini-tart shells cool completely on the baking sheet (about one hour).

3. While the crust is cooling, bring the apple cider, palm sugar, lemon zest, lemon juice, cinnamon stick, vanilla bean, vanilla seeds, peppercorns, cloves, and salt to a boil in a medium saucepan, stirring to dissolve the palm sugar (about 5 minutes). Add the pears and return to a brief simmer, then reduce the heat to low, cover, and poach the pears, turning them occasionally, until tender and a skewer can be inserted into each pears with little resistance (10 to 20 minutes). Remove the pot from the heat and let the pears cool in the poaching liquid, about one hour.

4. Preheat the oven again to 350°F.

5. Pulse the almonds, palm sugar, and salt together in a food processor until finely ground, about 1 minute. Add the egg and extracts and process until combined (about 10 seconds). Add the coconut oil and process until no lumps remain (about 30 seconds). Spread the mixture evenly into the cooled tart shell, or spoon evenly into mini-tart cups.

6. Remove the cooled pears from the poaching liquid and pat them dry thoroughly with paper towels. Slice and arrange the apple halves over the tart (quarter of a pear, sliced, per two mini-tarts). Bake the tart(s) on the baking sheet until the almond filling is puffed, browned, and firm to the touch (about 45 minutes for the full-size tart, and 15 to 20 minutes for the mini-tarts), rotating the baking sheet halfway through baking. Transfer the baking sheet to a wire rack to cool.

7. Melt the fruit jam in a small saucepan over medium-high heat, stirring occasionally to smooth out any lumps. Using a pastry brush, dab the melted fruit jam over the fruit. To serve, remove the outer metal ring of the tart pan, slide a thin metal spatula between the tart and pan bottom, and carefully slide the tart

onto a serving platter or cutting board. For mini-tarts, gently remove them from their cups and place on a serving platter.

Making the Tart(s) Ahead

The tart dough can be made ahead, as instructed in the original recipe. The poached pears, submerged in the poaching liquid, can be refrigerated in an airtight container for up to three days. The almond filling can also be refrigerated in an airtight container for up to three days. Once baked, the tart can be wrapped loosely with plastic wrap and held at room temperature for up to four hours before serving.

Baked Raspberry Tart

MAKES ONE NINE-INCH TART OR THIRTEEN FLUTED MINI-TARTS

Ingredients

1 recipe Classic Tart Dough (page 135)

6 tablespoons coconut oil, cut into 6 pieces

1 large egg

1 large egg white

½ cup palm sugar

¼ teaspoon salt

1 teaspoon vanilla extract

1 teaspoon kirsch or framboise (optional)

¼ teaspoon grated fresh lemon zest

1½ teaspoons fresh lemon juice

2 tablespoons coconut flour

2 tablespoons coconut milk

2 cups raspberries

Preparation

1. Roll the dough out to an eleven-inch circle on a lightly floured counter and fit into a nine-inch tart pan with a removable bottom, or press dough evenly into thirteen fluted mini-tart cups. Set the tart pan or mini-tart cups on a large plate and freeze the tart shell for 30 minutes.

2. Adjust an oven rack to the middle position and preheat the oven to 375°F. Set the tart pan or mini-tart cups on a large baking sheet. Bake until the tart shell is golden brown and set (about 30 minutes for full-size tart, or 10 to 15 minutes for mini-tarts), rotating the baking sheet halfway through baking. Transfer the baking sheet to a wire rack and let the tart shell or mini-tart shells cool completely on the baking sheet (about one hour).

3. Melt the coconut oil in a small saucepan over medium heat. Set aside to cool slightly.

4. In a medium bowl, whisk the egg and egg white together until combined. Vigorously whisk in the palm sugar and salt. Whisk in the coconut oil, vanilla, kirsch or framboise (if using), lemon zest, and the lemon juice. Lastly, whisk in the coconut flour, followed by the coconut milk, until well combined.

5. Distribute the raspberries in a single layer in the bottom of the cooled tart shell or mini-tart cups. Pour the filling mixture evenly over the raspberries. Bake the tart on the baking sheet until the filling is set (the center should not jiggle when

shaken) and the surface is puffed and deep golden brown (about 30 minutes), rotating the baking sheet halfway through baking.

6. Let the tart(s) cool completely on the baking sheet (about one and a half hours). To serve, remove the outer metal ring of the tart pan, slide a thin metal spatula between the tart and tart pan bottom, and carefully slide the tart onto a serving platter or cutting board. If using mini-tart cups, carefully pull edges of tart away from cups and gently remove the tart.

Making the Tart(s) Ahead
The tart dough can be made ahead, as instructed in the original recipe. Once baked and cooled, the tart can be wrapped loosely with plastic wrap and held at room temperature for up to four hours before serving.

Cranberry-Pecan Tart

Ingredients

1 recipe Classic Tart Dough (page 135)

¼ cup water

1 cup palm sugar

⅔ cup coconut milk

3 tablespoons coconut oil, cut into ½-inch pieces

½ teaspoon vanilla extract

½ teaspoon fresh lemon juice

⅛ teaspoon salt

1¼ cups pecans, toasted and chopped coarse

1½ cups cranberries, fresh or frozen (thawed)

Preparation

1. Roll the dough out to an eleven-inch circle on a lightly floured counter and fit into a nine-inch tart pan with a removable bottom, or press dough evenly into thirteen fluted mini-tart cups. Set the tart pan or mini-tart cups on a large plate and freeze the tart shell for 30 minutes.

2. Adjust an oven rack to the middle position and preheat the oven to 375°F. Set the tart pan or mini-tart cups on a large baking sheet. Bake until the tart shell is golden brown and set (about 30 minutes for full-size tart, or 10 to 15 minutes for mini-tarts), rotating the baking sheet halfway through baking. Transfer the baking sheet to a wire rack and let the tart shell or mini-tart shells cool completely on the baking sheet (about one hour).

3. Reduce the oven temperature to 325°F. Measure the water into a medium saucepan, then pour the palm sugar into the center of the pan (don't let it hit the pan sides). Gently stir the palm sugar with a clean spatula to wet it thoroughly. Bring to a boil over medium-high heat and cook, without stirring, until the palm sugar has dissolved completely and the liquid has a faint golden color.

4. Reduce the heat to medium-low and continue to cook, stirring occasionally, until the caramel turns a dark amber color (1 to 3 minutes). Remove from heat and slowly whisk in the coconut milk until combined (the mixture will bubble and steam vigorously). Stir in the coconut oil, vanilla, lemon juice, and salt until combined. Lastly, stir in the pecans and cranberries and mix gently to coat.

5. Pour the caramel mixture into the tart shell or baked mini-tart shells. Bake the tart on the baking sheet until the filling is set (25 to 30 minutes). It should not jiggle when shaken.
6. Let the tart(s) cool completely on the baking sheet (one and a half hours). To serve, remove the outer metal ring of the tart pan, slide a thin metal spatula between the tart and tart pan bottom, and carefully slide the tart onto a serving platter or cutting board. If using mini-tart cups, carefully pull edges of tart away from cups and gently remove the tart.

Making the Tart(s) Ahead

The tart dough can be made ahead, as instructed in the original recipe. Once baked and cooled, the tart can be wrapped loosely with plastic wrap and held at room temperature for up to four hours before serving.

Linzertorte

Ingredients

Tart Dough
1 cup hazelnuts, toasted

½ cup slivered almonds, toasted

½ cup palm sugar

½ teaspoon salt

1 teaspoon grated fresh lemon zest

½ teaspoon ground cinnamon

⅛ teaspoon ground allspice

¾ cup almond flour

¾ cup coconut flour

12 tablespoons coconut oil, cut into ¼-inch pieces and chilled

1 large egg

1 teaspoon vanilla extract

Filling
1¼ cups paleo raspberry jam (page 221)

1 tablespoon fresh lemon juice

1 tablespoon coconut milk

Palm sugar, for sprinkling (optional)

Preparation
1. Adjust an oven rack to the middle position and preheat the oven to 350°F.
2. Pulse the nuts, palm sugar, and salt together in a food processor until very finely ground (about 18 pulses). Add the lemon zest, cinnamon, and allspice and pulse to combine. Add the flour and pulse again to combine. Scatter the coconut oil pieces over the top and pulse until the mixture resembles coarse cornmeal (about 15 pulses).

3. In a small bowl, whisk the egg and vanilla together. With the food processor running, add the egg mixture to the nut mixture through the feed tube, then continue to pulse until the dough forms a large ball (about 10 pulses).

4. Divide dough into two equal parts. Tear one piece of the dough into walnut-size pieces and then pat it into an eleven-inch tart pan with a removable bottom, pressing it up the sides of the pan. Lay plastic wrap over the dough and smooth out any bumps using the palm of your hand. Set the tart pan on a large plate and freeze for 30 minutes.

5. Roll the second piece of dough into a twelve-inch square between two large sheets of floured parchment paper. Transfer to a baking sheet and refrigerate until firm (about 15 minutes). Remove the top layer of parchment and trim the edges of the dough, then cut into ten three-quarter-inch wide strips (you will have extra dough). Cover parchment and freeze until firm (about 20 minutes).

6. Set the tart pan on a large baking sheet. Bake until the tart shell is golden brown and set (about 30 minutes), rotating the baking sheet halfway through baking. Transfer the baking sheet to a wire rack. Let the tart shell cool on the baking sheet while making the filling.

7. Stir the raspberry jam and lemon juice together, then spread the mixture evenly over the bottom of the cooled tart shell. Remove the dough strips from the freezer, loosen the parchment on the top, then invert and loosen the other piece of parchment. Create a big X in the center of the tart using two strips of dough. Continue to lay eight more strips of dough on the tart to form a lattice. Press the ends of the strips against the rim of the tart pan to trim.

TO FORM LATTICE PATTERN: The dough will be too soft to weave, but you can still create the illusion of a woven crust with this method

- Crisscross two strips of dough to form an X over the center of the tart.
- Place four strips around the edges parallel to the central strips (looks like a box around the edge, with ends overlapping).
- Place the final four strips on the tart between the center X and outer strips (overlap the ends).
- Press the excess dough against the rim of the pan to trim.

1. Gently brush the lattice strips with the coconut milk and sprinkle with the palm sugar (if desired). Bake the tart on the baking sheet until the crust is a deep golden brown (about 50 minutes), rotating the baking sheet halfway through baking.

2. Let the tart(s) cool completely on the baking sheet (about two and a half hours). To serve, remove the outer metal ring of the tart pan, slide a thin metal spatula between the tart and tart pan bottom, and carefully slide the tart onto a serving platter or cutting board.

Making the Tart(s) Ahead

The tart dough can be divided into two pieces, wrapped separately in plastic wrap, and refrigerated for up to two days or frozen for up to one month. Let the refrigerated or frozen dough sit on the counter until very soft before using. Once baked and cooled, the tart can be wrapped loosely with plastic wrap and held at room temperature for up to one day before serving.

Lemon Tart

Ingredients

1 recipe Classic Tart Dough (page 135)	⅔ cup fresh lemon juice (4 lemons)
7 large egg yolks	1 pinch salt
2 large eggs	4 tablespoons coconut oil, cut into 4 pieces
1 cup palm sugar	3 tablespoons coconut cream, chilled
¼ cup grated fresh lemon zest (4 lemons)	

Preparation

1. Roll the dough out to an eleven-inch circle on a lightly floured counter and fit into a nine-inch tart pan with a removable bottom, or press dough evenly into thirteen fluted mini-tart cups. Set the tart pan or mini-tart cups on a large plate and freeze the tart shell for 30 minutes.

2. Adjust an oven rack to the middle position and preheat the oven to 375°F. Set the tart pan or mini-tart cups on a large baking sheet. Bake until the tart shell is golden brown and set (about 30 minutes for full-size tart, or 10 to 15 minutes for mini-tarts), rotating the baking sheet halfway through baking. Transfer the baking sheet to a wire rack and let the tart shell or mini-tart shells cool on the baking sheet while making the filling.

3. Whisk the egg yolks and eggs together in a medium saucepan. Whisk in the palm sugar until combined, then stir in the lemon zest, lemon juice, and salt. Add the coconut oil and cook over medium-low heat, stirring constantly, until the mixture thickens slightly and registers 170°F on an instant-read thermometer (about 2 to 5 minutes).

4. Pour the lemon filling into the warm tart shell or individual mini-tart cups. Bake the tart on the baking sheet until the filling is shiny and opaque, and the center jiggles slightly when shaken (10 to 15 minutes). Let the tart(s) cool completely on the baking sheet (about one and a half hours). To serve, remove the outer metal ring, slide a metal spatula between the tart and the tart pan bottom, and

carefully slide tart onto a serving platter or cutting board, or carefully remove tarts from mini cups and place on serving platter.

Making the Tart(s) Ahead

The tart dough can be made ahead; however, the tart shell needs to be freshly baked and warm when adding the filling. Once baked and cooled, the tart can be wrapped loosely with plastic wrap and held at room temperature for up to four hours before serving.

Chocolate Truffle Tart

SERVES 8 TO 10 (MAKES ONE NINE-INCH TART OR THIRTEEN FLUTED MINI-TART CUPS)

Ingredients

1 recipe Classic Tart Dough (page 135)

1 cup coconut milk

12 ounces cacao nibs, finely chopped

6 tablespoons coconut oil, softened

1 tablespoon cognac

Preparation

1. Roll the dough out to an eleven-inch circle on a lightly floured counter and fit into a nine-inch tart pan with a removable bottom, or press dough evenly into thirteen fluted mini-tart cups. Set the tart pan or mini-tart cups on a large plate and freeze the tart shell for 30 minutes.

2. Adjust an oven rack to the middle position and preheat the oven to 375°F. Set the tart pan or mini-tart cups on a large baking sheet. Bake until the tart shell is golden brown and set (about 30 minutes for full-size tart, or 10 to 15 minutes for mini-tarts), rotating the baking sheet halfway through baking. Transfer the baking sheet to a wire rack and let the tart shell or mini-tart shells cool on the baking sheet while making the filling.

3. Bring the coconut milk to a brief simmer in a small saucepan over medium-high heat. Remove from heat, stir in the cacao nibs and coconut oil, cover the pan, and let stand until the cacao nibs are mostly melted (about 2 minutes). Gently stir the mixture until smooth, and then stir in the cognac.

4. Pour the filling into the tart shell or individual mini tart cups and refrigerate, uncovered, until the filling is firm (about two hours). To serve, remove the outer metal ring, slide a metal spatula between the tart and the tart pan bottom, and carefully slide tart onto a serving platter or cutting board, or carefully remove mini-tarts from cups and place on a serving platter.

To Make Ahead

The tart dough can be made ahead, as per the instructions in the original recipe. The baked tart shell can be cooled completely, wrapped tightly in plastic wrap, and stored at room temperature for up to two days. Once filled and chilled, the tart can be wrapped loosely with plastic wrap and refrigerated for up to one day.

Chocolate-Walnut Tart

MAKES ONE NINE-INCH TART OR THIRTEEN FLUTED MINI TARTS

Ingredients

1 recipe Classic Tart Dough (page 135)

Walnut Filling

¼ cup water

1 cup palm sugar

⅔ cup coconut milk

3 tablespoons coconut oil, cut into 3 pieces

½ teaspoon vanilla extract

½ teaspoon fresh lemon juice

⅛ teaspoon salt

¼ cup walnuts, toasted and coarsely chopped, for topping

1 cup walnuts, toasted and coarsely chopped, for filling

Chocolate Filling

2 large egg yolks

⅓ cup coconut cream

⅓ cup coconut milk

5 ounces cacao nibs, finely chopped

2 tablespoons coconut oil, cut into 2 pieces

Preparation

1. Roll the dough out to an eleven-inch circle on a lightly floured counter and fit into a nine-inch tart pan with a removable bottom, or press dough evenly into thirteen fluted mini-tart cups. Set the tart pan or mini-tart cups on a large plate and freeze the tart shell for 30 minutes.

2. Adjust an oven rack to the middle position and preheat the oven to 375°F. Set the tart pan or mini-tart cups on a large baking sheet. Bake until the tart shell

is golden brown and set (about 30 minutes for full-size tart, or 10 to 15 minutes for mini-tarts), rotating the baking sheet halfway through baking. Transfer the baking sheet to a wire rack and let the tart shell or mini-tart shells cool on the baking sheet while making the filling.

3. Reduce the oven temperature to 300°F.

4. Measure the water into a medium saucepan; pour the palm sugar into the center of the pan (don't let it hit the pan sides). Gently stir the palm sugar with a clean spatula to wet it thoroughly. Bring to a boil over medium-high heat and cook, without stirring, until the palm sugar has dissolved completely and the liquid has a faint golden color (6 to 10 minutes).

5. Reduce the heat to medium-low and continue to cook, stirring occasionally, until the caramel develops a dark amber color (1 to 3 minutes). Remove from the heat and slowly whisk in the coconut milk until combined (the mixture will bubble and steam vigorously). Stir in the coconut oil, vanilla, lemon juice, and salt.

6. Stir the cup of chopped walnuts into the caramel, then pour the caramel mixture into the tart shell or mini-tart cups. Refrigerate uncovered until the caramel is firm and does not run when the pan is tilted (about 20 minutes).

7. While the caramel sets, whisk the egg yolks and one tablespoon of the coconut cream together in a small bowl. Bring the coconut milk and remaining cream to a simmer in a small saucepan. Remove from the heat, stir in the cacao nibs and coconut oil, cover the pan, and let stand until the cacao nibs are mostly melted (about 2 minutes). Gently stir the mixture until smooth, then add in the egg yolk mixture, stirring to combine.

8. Pour the chocolate filling evenly over the chilled caramel in the tart shell or mini-tart cups and smooth to an even layer by tilting the pan. Bake the tart on the baking sheet until tiny bubbles are visible on surface and the chocolate layer is just set (about 25 minutes).

9. Transfer the baking sheet to a wire rack and sprinkle the ¼ cup of toasted walnut halves on top of the tart to garnish. Let the tart cool slightly on the baking sheet

for 30 minutes, then refrigerate, uncovered, until the chocolate is firm (about three hours).

10. To serve, remove the outer metal ring, slide a metal spatula between the tart and the tart pan bottom, then carefully slide the tart onto a serving platter or cutting board, or carefully remove tarts from mini-tart cups and set on a serving platter.

To Make Ahead

The tart dough can be made ahead, per the instructions in the original recipe. Once filled and chilled, the tart can be wrapped loosely with plastic wrap and refrigerated for up to one day.

Espresso Truffle Tart

Ingredients

1 recipe Classic Tart Dough

1 cup coconut milk

12 ounce cacao nibs, finely chopped

6 tablespoons coconut oil, softened

2 teaspoons instant espresso or instant coffee

Preparation

1. Roll the dough out to an eleven-inch circle on a lightly floured counter and fit into a nine-inch tart pan with a removable bottom, or press dough evenly into thirteen fluted mini-tart cups. Set the tart pan or mini-tart cups on a large plate and freeze the tart shell for 30 minutes.

2. Adjust an oven rack to the middle position and preheat the oven to 375°F. Set the tart pan or mini-tart cups on a large baking sheet. Bake until the tart shell is golden brown and set (about 30 minutes for full-size tart, or 10 to 15 minutes for mini-tarts), rotating the baking sheet halfway through baking. Transfer the baking sheet to a wire rack and let the tart shell or mini-tart shells cool on the baking sheet while making the filling.

3. Bring the coconut milk to a brief simmer in a small saucepan over medium-high heat. Remove from the heat, stir in the cacao nibs and coconut oil, cover the pan, and let stand until the cacao nibs are mostly melted (about 2 minutes). Gently stir the mixture until smooth, then add instant espresso.

4. Pour the filling into the tart shell or mini-tart cups and refrigerate uncovered until the filling is firm (about two hours). To serve, remove the outer metal ring, slide a metal spatula between the tart and the tart pan bottom, and carefully slide the tart onto a serving platter or cutting board, or carefully remove tarts from mini-tart cups and place on serving platter.

Making the Tart(s) Ahead

The tart dough can be made ahead, as per the instructions in the original recipe. The baked tart shell can be cooled completely, wrapped tightly in plastic wrap, and stored at room temperature for up to two days. Once filled and chilled, the tart can be wrapped loosely with plastic wrap and refrigerated for up to one day.

{ Fruit Desserts }

Apple Crisp   165

Strawberry Shortcakes   166

Fresh Blueberry Crumble   168

Fresh Peach Crisp   170

Fresh Fruit Cobbler with Soft Cookie
    topping   172

Skillet Apple Brown Betty   175

Summer Berry Gratin   176

Summer Berry Bake   179

Berry Dessert Pancake   180

Blueberry Buckle   182

Individual Blackberry-Walnut Buckles   185

Cider-Baked Apples with Dried
    Cranberries   186

Apple Crisp

SERVES 6

Ingredients

Topping

⅔ cup almond flour or meal

⅓ cup pecans, chopped

5 tablespoons palm sugar

¼ cup coconut flour

3 tablespoons coconut oil, melted and cooled

½ teaspoon ground cinnamon

⅛ teaspoon salt

Coconut oil for greasing eight-inch baking dish

Filling

4 pounds sweet apples, peeled, cored, and halved

1 cup apple cider

2 tablespoons palm sugar

¾ teaspoon ground cinnamon

2 teaspoons lemon juice, fresh squeezed

Preparation

1. Transfer almond flour/meal to a medium bowl and stir in remaining topping ingredients.

2. Adjust oven rack to upper-middle position and preheat oven to 400°F.

3. Cut half of apples into one-inch chunks. Slice remaining apples into quarter-inch-thick wedges.

4. Bring apple chunks, juice, palm sugar, and cinnamon to simmer in a twelve-inch nonstick skillet over medium heat. Cover and cook, stirring occasionally, until apples are tender (about 15 minutes). Transfer mixture into large bowl and mash smooth with a potato masher. Measure out and reserve one tablespoon of mashed apple for topping. Return remaining mashed apple mixture to skillet and add sliced apples. Cover and cook over medium heat until slices begin to soften (about 5 minutes). Remove from heat and stir in lemon juice.

5. Combine all topping ingredients in a medium bowl, stirring to mix. Add the reserved tablespoon of mashed apple and stir until topping becomes crumbly.

6. Scrape filling into eight-inch square coconut oil greased baking dish and smooth into an even layer. Sprinkle topping over filling. Bake until juices are bubbling and topping is a deep golden brown (about 25 minutes). Cool on a wire rack for about 15 minutes before serving warm.

Strawberry Shortcakes

SERVES 8

Ingredients

Biscuits

2 cups almond flour

¾ cup coconut flour

2 tablespoons palm sugar

2 teaspoons baking powder

¾ teaspoon salt

½ cup coconut milk

6 tablespoons coconut milk, chilled

1 large egg

4 tablespoons coconut oil, melted and hot

Coconut oil for greasing muffin tins

Strawberries

2½ pounds strawberries, hulled (8 cups)

½ cup honey

Preparation

1. Adjust oven rack to upper-middle position and preheat oven to 425°F. Grease small muffin tin. Whisk flours, four teaspoons palm sugar, baking powder, and salt together in large bowl. In separate bowl, whisk coconut milk and egg together, then stir in hot melted coconut oil until it forms small clumps. Stir coconut milk mixture into flour mixture until dough comes together and no dry bits remain.

2. Using a greased quarter-cup measure, scoop out and drop eight quantities of dough into eight small muffin tin spaces, spaced out about 1½ inches apart. Sprinkle remaining two teaspoons palm sugar over top. Bake shortcakes until golden brown and crisp (about 15 minutes), rotating sheet halfway through baking. Transfer muffin tin to wire rack and let cool for 15 minutes. Remove biscuits from tins.

3. Using a potato masher, crush three cups strawberries with honey in a large bowl. Thinly slice the remaining five cups of strawberries, then stir into mashed strawberries. Let sit at room temperature until honey has dissolved and berries are juicy (about 30 minutes).

4. Spoon berry mixture over shortcake bottoms.

Fresh Blueberry Crumble

SERVES 6 TO 8

Ingredients

Blueberry Fruit Filling

6 cups fresh blueberries

4 teaspoons tapioca flour

⅔ cup palm sugar

1 tablespoon fresh lemon juice

½ teaspoon cinnamon

Coconut oil for greasing baking dish

Crumble

1 cup almond flour

½ cup palm sugar

2 teaspoons vanilla extract

⅛ teaspoon salt

6 tablespoons coconut oil, cut into 6 pieces
and softened

½ cup sliced almonds

Preparation

1. Adjust the oven racks to the lower-middle and upper-middle positions and preheat the oven to 350°F. Grease an eight-inch square baking dish with coconut oil and set on a foil-lined rimmed baking sheet (for easy cleanup). Line another rimmed baking sheet with parchment paper.

2. Combine all of the filling ingredients in a large bowl. Transfer the fruit filling to the prepared baking dish and cover with foil.

3. Pulse the flour, ½ cup palm sugar, vanilla, and salt in a food processor until combined (about 5 pulses). Sprinkle the coconut oil and ¼ cup of the almonds over the top and process until the mixture clumps together into large crumbly balls (about 30 seconds). Sprinkle the remaining ¼ cup of almonds over the top and pulse to incorporate (about 2 pulses).

4. Turn the mixture out onto the parchment-lined baking sheet, breaking it into half-inch pieces (with some smaller loose bits), and spread into an even layer. Place the topping on the lower-middle oven rack and the fruit on the upper-middle oven rack. Bake until the topping is lightly browned and the fruit is warm at the edges and glistens (15 to 20 minutes).

5. Remove both the topping and the fruit from the oven. Uncover the fruit, stir gently, and sprinkle the crumb topping evenly over the top, breaking up any large pieces. Sprinkle with the remaining tablespoon of palm sugar.

6. Bake the crumble on the lower-middle oven rack until the topping is well browned and the fruit is bubbling around the edges (about 25 minutes), rotating the dish halfway through baking. Let the crumble cool for 10 minutes before serving.

Making the Crumble Ahead

The topping can be prebaked, then cooled and stored in an airtight container at room temperature for up to three days. The fruit filling can be assembled in the baking dish and held at room temperature for up to four hours before baking. To finish, bake the fruit by itself, then assemble topping and bake the crumble as directed.

Fresh Peach Crisp

SERVES 6 TO 8

Ingredients

Peach Fruit Filling

3 pounds peaches, peeled, halved, cored, and cut into 1½-inch chunks

1 tablespoon tapioca flour

2 to 4 tablespoons palm sugar

1 teaspoon fresh lemon juice

1 teaspoon vanilla extract

Coconut oil for greasing baking dish

Crisp

¾ cup almonds, toasted and chopped

½ cup almond flour

¼ cup palm sugar

2 tablespoons palm sugar

¼ teaspoon ground cinnamon

⅛ teaspoon ground nutmeg

⅛ teaspoon salt

5 tablespoons coconut oil, melted

Preparation

1. Adjust an oven rack to the middle position and preheat the oven to 400°F. Grease an eight-inch square baking dish with coconut oil and set on a foil-lined rimmed baking sheet (for easy cleanup).
2. Combine all peach fruit filling ingredients in a bowl. Transfer the fruit filling to the prepared baking dish, cover with foil, and bake the fruit until it is hot and has released its juices (20 to 25 minutes).
3. While the fruit is cooking, pulse the almonds, flour, palm sugar, cinnamon, nutmeg, and salt together in a food processor until the nuts are finely chopped (about 9 pulses). Add the coconut oil and pulse until the mixture resembles crumbly, wet sand (about 5 pulses). Transfer the mixture to a medium bowl and pinch between your fingers into small pea-sized pieces (with some smaller loose bits).
4. Remove the fruit from the oven, uncover, and stir gently. Sprinkle the topping evenly over the fruit. Bake the crisp until the topping is a deep golden brown

and the fruit is bubbling (about 15 minutes), rotating the dish halfway through baking. Let the crisp cool for 10 minutes before serving.

Making the Crisp Ahead

The topping can be transferred to an airtight contain and refrigerated for up to three days, or frozen for up to one month. If frozen, allow to thaw completely before using. The fruit filling can be assembled in the baking dish and held at room temperature for up to four hours before baking. To finish, bake as directed.

Fresh Fruit Cobbler with Soft Cookie Topping

Serves 8

Ingredients

Blackberry Fruit Filling

6 cups fresh blackberries, (or berry of choice) rinsed

1 tablespoon tapioca flour

⅔ cup palm sugar

1 teaspoon fresh lemon juice

1 teaspoon vanilla extract

Coconut oil for greasing baking dish

Soft Cookie

1½ cups almond flour

¼ cup plus 2 teaspoon palm sugar

1½ teaspoon baking powder

¼ teaspoon salt

¾ cup coconut oil coconut milk, chilled

6 tablespoons coconut oil, melted and slightly cooled

⅛ teaspoon ground cinnamon

Preparation

1. Adjust the oven racks to the lower-middle and upper-middle positions and preheat the oven to 350°F. Grease an eight-inch square baking dish with coconut oil and set on a foil-lined rimmed baking sheet (for easy cleanup). Line another rimmed baking sheet with parchment paper.

2. Combine all of the filling ingredients in a large bowl. Transfer the fruit filling to the prepared baking dish and cover with foil.

3. Whisk the flour, ¼ cup of the palm sugar, baking powder, baking soda, and salt together in a large bowl. In a medium bowl, stir the chilled coconut oil, coconut milk, and melted coconut oil together until the coconut oil forms small clumps. Stir the oil-milk mixture into the flour mixture with a rubber spatula until just incorporated and the dough begins to pull away from the sides of the bowl.

4. Using a greased quarter-cup measure, scoop and drop eight mounds of dough onto the parchment-lined baking sheet, spaced about one-and-a-half inches apart. Toss the remaining two teaspoons palm sugar with the cinnamon and sprinkle over the cookie tops. Bake the cookies until puffed and lightly browned on the bottom (about 10 minutes). Cookies will be flat and delicately tender.

5. Remove the cookies from the oven and set aside. Place the fruit in the oven and bake until it is hot and bubbling and has released its juices (20 to 30 minutes).
6. Remove the fruit from the oven, uncover, and stir gently. Arrange the cookies over the top. Let the cobbler cool for 10 minutes before serving.

Skillet Apple Brown Betty

Ingredients

bread crumbs

4 slices high-quality paleo sandwich bread, torn into quarters

4 tablespoons palm sugar

3 tablespoons coconut oil, cut into 3 pieces

Apples

½ cup palm sugar

¼ teaspoon ground ginger

¼ teaspoon ground cinnamon

3 tablespoons coconut oil

1½ pounds Granny Smith apples, peeled, cored, and cut into ½ inch pieces

1¼ cups apple cider

1 to 3 teaspoons fresh lemon juice (if apples are especially tart, omit the lemon juice)

Preparation

1. Pulse the bread, palm sugar, and coconut oil together in a food processor until coarsely ground (about 4 pulses). Transfer the crumbs to a twelve-inch nonstick skillet and toast over medium heat, stirring constantly, until the crumbs are deep golden brown (8 to 10 minutes). Transfer to a paper towel-lined plate and wipe out the skillet.

2. Combine the palm sugar, ginger, cinnamon, and salt in a small bowl. Melt 1½ tablespoons of the coconut oil in the skillet over high heat. Stir in half the apples and half of the palm sugar mixture. Spread the apples into an even layer and cook, stirring occasionally, until lightly browned (about 5 minutes). Transfer the apples to a medium bowl. Repeat with the remaining coconut oil, apples, and palm sugar mixture.

3. Combine all of the apples in the pan and add the apple cider. Cook until the apples are tender, but not mushy, and the liquid has reduced and is just beginning to thicken (2 to 4 minutes). Remove the skillet from the heat and stir in the lemon juice (if using) and ⅓ cup of the toasted breadcrumbs. Lightly press the apples into an even layer in the skillet and sprinkle evenly with the remaining toasted breadcrumbs. Spoon the warm apple brown betty into individual bowls and serve.

Summer Berry Gratin

SERVES 4 TO 6

Ingredients

4½ cups fresh summer berries
1 tablespoon palm sugar
1 tablespoon vanilla extract
1 pinch salt
3 large slices paleo bread, torn into quarters
¼ cup palm sugar
2 tablespoons coconut oil, softened
Pinch ground cinnamon

Preparation

1. Adjust an oven rack to the middle position and preheat the oven to 400°F.
2. Gently toss the berries with the palm sugar, vanilla, and salt, then spread into a 1½-quart casserole or gratin dish.
3. Pulse the bread, palm sugar, coconut oil, and cinnamon together in a food processor until the mixture resembles coarse crumbs (about 10 pulses). Sprinkle the crumbs evenly over the fruit.
4. Bake the gratin until the crumbs are a deep golden brown and the fruit is hot (15 to 20 minutes), rotating the dish halfway through baking. Let cool on a wire rack for 5 minutes before serving.

Summer Berry Bake

SERVES 4 TO 6

Ingredients

4 ounces coconut milk

1 tablespoon tapioca flour

¼ cup lemon juice

1 teaspoon lemon zest

¼ cup coconut milk

2 cups fresh raspberries

1 cup fresh blueberries

¼ cup palm sugar

Preparation

1. Adjust an oven rack seven inches from the broiler element and heat the broiler. Whisk the coconut milk, lemon juice, lemon zest, and tapioca flour together in a medium bowl until smooth. Place in a saucepan over medium high heat and bring to a boil, whisking continuously until thickened. Remove from heat.

2. Scatter the berries in a 1-quart, broiler-safe gratin dish or tart pan. Spoon the coconut milk mixture over the berries and gently spread it to cover the berries completely in an even layer. Sprinkle the palm sugar over the top.

3. Broil until the palm sugar is bubbly and evenly caramelized (2 to 4 minutes). Serve immediately.

Berry Dessert Pancake

Ingredients

1 cup almond flour

½ teaspoon salt

1 cup coconut milk

1 large egg

½ teaspoon vanilla extract

4 tablespoons coconut oil

2 cups fresh summer berries

¼ cup palm sugar

2 tablespoons palm sugar

Preparation

1. Adjust an oven rack to the lower-middle position and preheat the oven to 375°F.
2. Whisk the flour and salt together in a large bowl. In a separate medium bowl, whisk the coconut milk, egg, and vanilla together. Make a well in the center of the flour mixture, and pour in the coconut milk mixture. Whisk together until combined (a few small lumps may remain).
3. Melt the coconut oil in a twelve-inch ovenproof skillet over medium heat. Swirl the coconut oil to coat the pan fully, then pour the batter into the center of the skillet and let it spread into an even layer. Working quickly, scatter the berries over the batter, leaving a one-inch border around the edge. Sprinkle the palm sugar over the berries (leaving the border around the edge clean).
4. Transfer skillet to the oven and bake the pancake until the edges are puffed and deep golden brown (10 to 15 minutes), rotating the skillet halfway through baking. Slide the pancake onto a serving platter, cut into wedges, and serve immediately.

Blueberry Buckle

SERVES 8 TO 10

Ingredients

Streusel Topping
½ cup almond flour

⅔ cup palm sugar

¼ teaspoon ground cinnamon

Pinch salt

4 tablespoons coconut oil, softened

Cake
1½ cups almond flour

1½ teaspoons baking powder

10 tablespoons coconut oil, softened

⅔ cup palm sugar

½ teaspoon salt

½ teaspoon grated fresh lemon zest

2 large eggs, room temperature

1½ teaspoons vanilla extract

4 cups fresh blueberries

Coconut oil for greasing cake pan

Preparation

1. Adjust an oven rack to the lower-middle position and preheat the oven to 350°F. Grease and flour a nine-inch round cake pan, then line bottom with parchment paper.

2. Whisk the flour, palm sugar, cinnamon, and salt together in a large bowl. Beat in the coconut oil with an electric mixer on low speed until the mixture resembles moist crumbs.

3. In a small bowl, whisk the flour and baking powder together. In a separate large bowl, beat the coconut oil, palm sugar, salt, and lemon zest together with an electric mixer on medium speed until light and fluffy. Beat in the eggs, one at a time, until combined (about 30 seconds), followed by the vanilla.

4. Reduce the mixer speed to low and slowly add in the flour mixture until just incorporated (the batter will be extremely thick and heavy). Gently fold in the blueberries with a rubber spatula.

5. Scrape the batter into the prepared pan, smooth the top, and gently tap the pan on the counter to settle the batter. Sprinkle the streusel evenly over top. Bake the

buckle until it is a deep golden brown and a toothpick inserted into the center comes out with a few crumbs attached (about 55 minutes), rotating the pan halfway through baking.

6. Let the cake cool in the pan for 10 minutes (the cake will fall slightly as it cools). Run a small knife around the edge of the cake and flip it out onto a large plate (not the serving platter). Peel off the parchment paper, flip the cake right-side up onto a serving platter, and let cool until just warm or to room temperature (at least one hour) before serving.

Individual Blackberry-Walnut Buckles

SERVES 8

Ingredients

¾ cup palm sugar

½ cup walnuts, toasted and chopped coarse

4 tablespoons coconut oil, softened

¼ teaspoon salt

⅓ cup coconut milk

2 large eggs

1 teaspoon vanilla extract

¾ cup almond flour

½ teaspoon baking powder

3 cups fresh blackberries

Coconut oil for greasing ramekins

Preparation

1. Adjust an oven rack to the middle position and preheat the oven to 375°F. Grease eight six-ounce ramekins with coconut oil and place on a rimmed baking sheet.

2. Process the palm sugar, ¼ cup of the walnuts, coconut oil, and salt together in a food processor until finely ground (10 to 15 seconds). With the processor running, add the cream, eggs, and vanilla through the feed tube and continue to process until smooth (about 5 seconds). Add the flour and baking powder and pulse until just incorporated (about 5 pulses).

3. Transfer the batter to a large bowl and gently fold in the blackberries. Spoon the batter into the prepared ramekins and sprinkle with the remaining ¼ cup walnuts.

4. Bake the buckles until they are golden and begin to pull away from the sides of the ramekins (25 to 30 minutes), rotating the baking sheet halfway through baking. Let cool on a wire rack for 10 minutes before serving.

Cider-Baked Apples with Dried Cranberries

SERVES 4

Ingredients

4 large apples
½ cup dried cranberries or cherries
¼ cup palm sugar
¼ teaspoon ground cinnamon
1½ cups apple cider
2 cinnamon sticks
¼ cup walnuts, toasted and finely chopped
Coconut oil for greasing baking dish

Preparation

1. Adjust an oven rack to the middle position and preheat the oven to 375°F. Using a vegetable peeler, remove a strip of apple peel from the top of each apple. Remove the stem and core of each apple using a melon baller, being careful not the cut all the way through the blossom end.

2. Place the apples in a greased eight-inch square baking dish. Divide ¼ cup of the dried cranberries evenly among the apple cavities. Mix the palm sugar and cinnamon together in a small bowl and then sprinkle in and around the apples. Add the cider, cinnamon sticks, and the remaining ¼ cup of dried cranberries to the baking dish.

3. Bake the apples until they are tender when pierced with a paring knife or skewer (45 to 55 minutes), brushing the apples with the cider several times during baking. (Be careful not to overbake; the apples or the skins will split.)

4. Transfer the apples to individual serving bowls. Pour the cooking liquid with cinnamon sticks and cranberries into a small saucepan, bring to simmer over medium-high heat, and cook until it thickens and measures about one cup (7 to 10 minutes). Spoon some of the sauce over each apple, sprinkle with the walnuts, and serve, passing the remaining sauce separately.

{ Milkshakes, Puddings, and Mousses }

Chocolate Milkshake   191

Mocha Frappe   192

Chocolate Mousse   195

Chilled Lemon Mousse with
    Raspberry Sauce   196

Chocolate Pudding   199

Chocolate Banana Pudding   200

Vanilla Pudding   203

Strawberry Vanilla Pudding   204

Peach Vanilla Pudding   207

Bread Pudding   208

Rich and Creamy Banana Pudding   211

Chocolate Milkshake

Ingredients

⅓ cup coconut milk

3 ice cubes

1 teaspoon water

½ teaspoon cacao powder

½ tablespoon honey or palm sugar

¼ teaspoon vanilla extract

Preparation

1. Heat water, cacao powder, and honey in a small saucepan until boiling. Whisk in palm sugar, stirring until sugar is dissolved and mixture is slightly thickened. Remove from heat and cool to room temperature.

2. Process coconut milk, ice cubes, cacao sauce, and vanilla together in a blender until smooth (about 20 seconds). Pour into a chilled sixteen-ounce drinking glass and serve with a straw.

Mocha Frappe

SERVES 1

Ingredients

⅓ cup coconut milk

2 teaspoons instant espresso powder

1½ cups ice cubes

2 teaspoons palm sugar

¼ teaspoon vanilla extract

1 cup coconut milk, chilled

Preparation

1. Blend coconut milk and espresso powder together in blender until espresso dissolves (about 5 seconds). Add ice, palm sugar, chilled coconut milk, and vanilla and blend until incorporated (about 10 seconds). Pour into a chilled sixteen-ounce drinking glass and serve with a straw, if desired.

Chocolate Mousse

SERVES 6

Ingredients

4 ounces cacao nibs

⅓ cup non-dairy white chocolate chips

2 tablespoons cacao powder

6 tablespoons, plus ⅓ cup water

1 teaspoon vanilla extract

⅓ cup palm sugar

3 large egg whites, room temperature

¼ teaspoon lemon juice

Preparation

1. Combine cacao nibs, white chocolate chips, cacao powder, six tablespoons water, and vanilla in a medium heatproof bowl set over a large saucepan of barely simmering water, making sure the water does not touch the bottom of the bowl. Heat mixture, whisking often, until chocolate is melted and mixture is smooth (about 2 minutes). Set aside and cool slightly.

2. Bring remaining ⅓ cup water and palm sugar to a boil in a small saucepan over medium-high heat and cook until mixture is slightly thickened and syrupy (3 to 4 minutes). Remove from heat and cover to keep warm.

3. Using a stand mixer fitted with a whisk, whip egg whites and lemon juice together on medium-low speed until foamy (about 1 minute). Increase speed to medium-high and whip until soft peaks form (2 to 3 minutes).

4. Reduce speed to medium and slowly add hot syrup, avoiding whisk and sides of bowl. Increase mixer speed to medium-high and continue to whip until meringue has cooled slightly (just warm) and is very thick and shiny (2 to 5 minutes).

5. Gently whisk ⅓ of the meringue into the chocolate mixture until combined, then gently whisk in remaining meringue. Divide mousse evenly among six four-ounce ramekins or pudding cups. Cover tightly with plastic wrap and refrigerate until set (at least three hours). Serve within six hours.

Chilled Lemon Mousse with Raspberry Sauce

SERVES 6

Ingredients

Sauce

¾ cup raspberries

2 tablespoons honey

2 tablespoons water

1 pinch salt

Mousse

2½ tablespoons tapioca flour

¾ cup coconut milk

1½ teaspoons grated lemon zest

3 tablespoons lemon juice

1 teaspoon vanilla extract

⅛ teaspoon salt

3 large egg whites

6 tablespoons palm sugar

Preparation

1. Simmer all sauce ingredients in a medium saucepan over medium heat until honey is dissolved (2 to 4 minutes). Transfer sauce mixture to a blender and process until smooth (about 15 seconds). Strain the sauce through a fine-mesh strainer; you should end up with ½ cup of sauce. Spoon sauce into six four-ounce ramekins and refrigerate until chilled (about 20 minutes).

2. While the sauce is chilling, whisk tapioca flour, coconut milk, lemon zest and juice, vanilla, and salt together in a large metal bowl until smooth. Set bowl over a large saucepan of barely simmering water, making sure that the water does not touch the bottom of the bowl. Whisk until thickened. Immediately pour through a fine mesh strainer. Chill strained mousse for 10 minutes.

3. Spoon mousse evenly into chilled ramekins on top of sauce, cover tightly with plastic wrap, and refrigerate until chilled and set (six to eight hours). Serve chilled.

Chocolate Pudding

SERVES 4

Ingredients

½ cup palm sugar

2½ tablespoons tapioca flour

2 tablespoons cacao powder

⅛ teaspoon salt

2½ cups coconut milk

2 ounces cacao nibs, chopped

2 teaspoons vanilla extract

Preparation

1. Combine palm sugar, tapioca flour, cacao powder, and salt together in bowl. Whisk coconut milk and palm sugar mixture together in medium saucepan. Add cacao nibs and bring to a boil over medium heat, whisking constantly. Reduce the heat to low and cook, whisking constantly, until mixture becomes thick and glossy (about 3 minutes).

2. Remove from heat and stir in vanilla. Strain mixture through a fine-mesh strainer into a bowl. Place plastic wrap directly on surface of pudding to prevent a skin from forming. Refrigerate until well chilled (at least four hours, or up to two days). Gently stir pudding before serving.

Chocolate-Banana Pudding

Serves 4

Ingredients

½ cup palm sugar

2½ tablespoons tapioca flour

2 tablespoons cacao powder

⅛ teaspoon salt

2 cups coconut milk

1 ripe banana

2 ounces cacao nibs, chopped

2 teaspoons vanilla extract

Preparation

1. Combine palm sugar, tapioca flour, cacao powder, and salt together in bowl. Whisk coconut milk and palm sugar mixture together in a medium saucepan. Mash banana with a fork in a small bowl and add to saucepan. Add cacao nibs, mix well to combine, and bring mixture to a boil over medium heat, whisking constantly. Reduce heat to low and cook, whisking constantly, until mixture becomes thick and glossy (about 3 minutes).

2. Remove from heat and stir in vanilla. Strain mixture through a fine-mesh strainer into a bowl. Place plastic wrap directly on surface of pudding to prevent a skin from forming. Refrigerate until well chilled (at least four hours, or up to two days). Gently stir pudding before serving.

Vanilla Pudding

Ingredients

4 cups coconut milk
½ cup palm sugar
1 teaspoon vanilla
3 to 4 tablespoons of tapioca flour

Preparation

1. Combine all ingredients in a saucepan and bring to a boil over medium-high heat, whisking constantly. Reduce heat to low and cook, whisking constantly, until mixture becomes thick and glossy (about 3 minutes).

2. Remove from heat and stir in vanilla. Strain mixture through a fine-mesh strainer into a bowl. Place plastic wrap directly on surface of pudding to prevent a skin from forming. Refrigerate until well chilled (at least four hours, or up to two days). Gently stir pudding before serving.

Strawberry-Vanilla Pudding

Ingredients

3½ cups coconut milk

½ cup palm sugar

½ cup strawberries, stems removed and mashed

1 teaspoon vanilla

3 to 4 tablespoons of tapioca flour

Preparation

1. Combine all ingredients in a saucepan and bring to a boil over medium-high heat, whisking constantly. Reduce heat to low and cook, whisking constantly, until mixture becomes thick and glossy (about 3 minutes). Remove from heat. Add strawberries to pudding and stir to combine. Stir in vanilla.

2. Place plastic wrap directly on surface of pudding to prevent a skin from forming. Refrigerate until well chilled (at least four hours, or up to two days). Gently stir pudding before serving.

Peach-Vanilla Pudding

Ingredients

3½ cups coconut milk
½ cup palm sugar
½ cup peaches, peeled, seeded, and chopped
1 teaspoon vanilla
3 to 4 tablespoons of tapioca flour

Preparation

1. Combine all ingredients in a saucepan and bring to a boil over medium-high heat, whisking constantly. Reduce heat to low and cook, whisking constantly, until mixture becomes thick and glossy (about 3 minutes). Remove from heat and add peaches to pudding, stirring to combine. Stir in vanilla.

2. Place plastic wrap directly on surface of pudding to prevent a skin from forming. Refrigerate until well chilled (at least four hours, or up to two days). Gently stir pudding before serving.

Bread Pudding

SERVES

Ingredients

---

2 cups skim coconut milk

3 large eggs

5 tablespoons palm sugar

3 tablespoons tapioca flour

2 teaspoons vanilla extract

¼ teaspoon salt

¼ teaspoon ground cinnamon

12 slices prune-nut bread (see page 97), cut into three-quarter inch pieces

---

Preparation

1. Adjust oven rack to middle position and preheat oven to 375°F. Lightly spray an eight-inch square baking dish with vegetable oil spray.

2. Whisk coconut milk, eggs, ¼ cup of palm sugar, tapioca flour, vanilla extract, and salt together in large bowl until combined. Gently stir in bread. Let mixture sit, tossing occasionally, until liquid is mostly absorbed (about 10 minutes).

3. Combine remaining tablespoon of palm sugar with cinnamon in small bowl. Transfer soaked bread mixture to the prepared baking dish and sprinkle with cinnamon-palm sugar. Bake bread pudding until just set and surface is golden brown (35 to 40 minutes). Let bread pudding cool on wire rack for 15 minutes. Serve.

Rich and Creamy Banana Pudding

SERVES 12

Ingredients

7 slightly underripe large bananas

4 cups coconut milk

½ cup palm sugar

1 teaspoon vanilla

3½ tablespoons of tapioca flour

Ingredients

1. Preheat oven to 350°F. Place bananas with skin intact on a baking sheet and place in oven. Bake until skin blackens, about 5 minutes. Remove from oven and cool until skin can be comfortably peeled without burning your hands. Peel bananas. Mash 3 of the bananas and set aside.

2. Combine mashed bananas, coconut milk, palm sugar, vanilla and tapioca flour in a saucepan and bring to a boil over medium-high heat, whisking constantly. Reduce heat to low and cook, whisking constantly, until mixture becomes thick and glossy (about 3 minutes).

3. Remove from heat and stir in vanilla. Strain mixture through a fine-mesh strainer into a bowl. Place plastic wrap directly on surface of pudding to prevent a skin from forming. Refrigerate until well chilled (at least four hours, or up to two days). Gently stir pudding before serving.

4. Slice remaining bananas to a quarter-inch thickness and layer with pudding in bowls. Start with a pudding layer, then add bananas, and repeat, ending with pudding on top.

{ Frostings and Jam }

Chocolate Frosting   215

Chocolate Frosting with orange essence   216

Coconut Frosting   218

Pecan Coconut Frosting   219

Fruit Jam   221

Chocolate Frosting

SERVES 10

Ingredients

2 avocados, peeled and pitted

½ cup cacao powder

½ cup honey

2 tablespoons coconut oil

1 teaspoon vanilla extract

½ teaspoon salt

Preparation

1. Blend avocados, cacao powder, honey, coconut oil, vanilla extract, and salt together in a food processor until smooth.

Chocolate Frosting with Orange Essence

SERVES 10

Ingredients

2 avocados, peeled and pitted

½ cup cacao powder

½ cup honey

2 tablespoons coconut oil

1 teaspoon vanilla extract

½ teaspoon salt

½ teaspoon orange extract

Preparation

1. Blend avocados, cacao powder, honey, coconut oil, vanilla and orange extracts, and salt together in a food processor until smooth.

Coconut Frosting

Ingredients

½ cup honey

2 tablespoons coconut oil, melted and cooled

4 tablespoons coconut milk

1 cup unsweetened, shredded coconut

Preparation

1. In a medium bowl, whisk the honey, melted coconut oil, and coconut milk together, then stir in the coconut.

Pecan Coconut Frosting

Ingredients

½ cup honey

2 tablespoons coconut oil, melted and cooled

4 tablespoons coconut milk

1 cup unsweetened shredded coconut

½ cup pecans, chopped

Preparation

1. In a medium bowl, whisk the honey, melted coconut oil, and coconut milk together, then stir in the coconut and pecans.

Fruit Jam

MAKES EIGHT OUNCES OF JAM

Ingredients

3 cups frozen berries (blueberries, strawberries, raspberries, apricots, blackberries, etc.)
⅔ cup honey
1 to 2 tablespoons of fresh lemon juice (juice of about 1 lemon)

Preparation

1. Place a small saucepan over medium heat. Add frozen berries or fruit and simmer until juices begin to release from the fruit. Add honey and lemon juice. Mix well and simmer for 5 to 7 minutes, then reduce heat to medium-low heat and simmer for another 5 to 7 minutes, stirring occasionally. Reduce heat to low and simmer until desired thickness is achieved. Thickness of the jam will vary with the amount of cooking time.

CHEF'S NOTE: Use one kind of berry or combine the types you use. Feel free to add spices like ginger, ground cayenne, or black pepper, etc. to add a little kick or twist to your jams.

{ Conversions and Equivalencies }

Ibelieve cooking is equal parts science and art, and your physical location has a lot to do with how to prepare a recipe. That is to say, the locations from which your ingredients originate have an impact on the overall recipe formulation. Ingredients from different parts of the world may vary slightly, and I cannot promise that almond flour from one supplier will yield exactly the same result as another. I can, however, offer guidelines for converting weights and measurements. I also recommend that you rely on your individual judgment (here's the art part) when preparing the recipes. If a recipe isn't behaving exactly as I describe it should, adjust the moisture, flours or palm sugar levels until you get it right. The recipes in this book were developed using standard U.S. measures. The following charts offer equivalents for U.S., metric, and imperial (U.K.) measures. All conversions are approximate and have been rounded up or down to the nearest whole number.

EXAMPLE: 1 teaspoon = 4.9292 milliliters (rounded up to 5 milliliters)
1 ounce = 28.3495 grams (rounded down to 28 grams)

VOLUME CONVERSIONS U.S. TO METRIC
1 teaspoon = 5 milliliters
2 teaspoons = 10 milliliters
1 tablespoon = 15 milliliters
2 tablespoons = 30 milliliters
¼ cup = 59 milliliters
⅓ cup = 79 milliliters
½ cup = 118 milliliters
¾ cup = 177 milliliters
1 cup = 237 milliliters
1¼ cups = 296 milliliters
1½ cups = 355 milliliters

2 cups (1 pint) = 473 milliliters

2½ cups = 591 milliliters

3 cups = 710 milliliters

4 cups (1 quart) = 0.946 liter

1.06 quarts = 1 liter

4 quarts (1 gallon) = 3.8 liters

VOLUME CONVERSIONS U.S. TO METRIC
Ounces to Grams

½ = 14

¾ = 21

1 = 28

1½ = 43

2 = 57

2½ = 71

3 = 85

3½ = 99

4 = 113

4½ = 128

5 = 142

6 = 170

7 = 198

8 = 227

9 = 255

10 = 283

12 = 340

16 (1 pound) = 454

OVEN TEMPERATURES: FAHRENHEIT TO CELSIUS AND TO GAS MARK (IMPERIAL)

225 = 105 = ¼

250 = 120 = ½

275 = 135 = 1

300 = 150 = 2

325 = 165 = 3

350 = 180 = 4

375 = 190 = 5

400 = 200 = 6

425 = 220 = 7

450 = 230 = 8

475 = 245 = 9

Subtract 32°F from the Fahrenheit reading, and then divide the result by 1.8 to find the Celsius reading.

Temperature conversion example:

175°F − 32 = 143°

143° ÷ 1.8 = 79.44°C, rounded down to 79°C

{ Index }

Almond Blossom Cookies, 32–33
Almond Butter Cookies, 39
Almond Butter Pie, 130
Almond flour, ix
Almond Fudge Bars, 76–77
Almond Meal Cake With Broiled Icing, 100–101
Almond Prune Cookies, 4
Almond Raisin Cookies, 3
Almonds
    Almond Blossom Cookies, 32–33
    Almond Butter Cookies, 39
    Apricot Squares, 80–81
    Fresh Blueberry Crumble, 168–169
    Fresh Peach Crisp, 170–171
    Ginger-Almond Cookies, 7
    Italian Almond Cake, 103
    Lebkuchen, 28–29
    Linzertorte, 149–151
    Nutty Almond Cookies, 11
    Orange Almond Cookies, 8
    Peach Squares, 78–79
    Poached Almond Tart, 138–139
    Poached Pear and Almond Tart, 140–143
    Strawberry Squares, 82–83
Apple cider
    Apple Crisp, 165
    Applesauce Snack Cake, 90–91
    Cider-Baked Apples with Dried Cranberries, 186
    Fig Bars, 84–85
    Poached Apple Tart, 138–139
    Poached Pear and Almond Tart, 140–141
    Skillet Apple Brown Betty, 175
Apple Crisp, 165
Apples
    Apple Crisp, 165
    Applesauce Snack Cake, 90–91
    Cider-Baked Apples with Dried Cranberries, 186
    Poached Apple Tart, 138–139
    Skillet Apple Brown Betty, 175
Applesauce Snack Cake, 90–91
Apricot Squares, 80–81
Arrowroot flour, xi
Avocados
    Chocolate Frosting, 215

    Chocolate Frosting with Orange
    Essence, 216

Baked Raspberry Tart, 144–145
Baking powder, x
Baking soda, x
Banana Pudding, 211
Bananas
    Chocolate-Banana Pudding, 200
    Individual Bananas Foster Cakes, 104–105
    Rich and Creamy Banana Pudding, 211
Bananas Foster Cakes, 104–105
Bars
    Almond Fudge Bars, 76–77
    Apricot Squares, 80–81
    Blondies, 75
    Fig Bars, 84–85
    Key Lime Bars, 72
    Lemon Squares, 71
    Peach Squares, 78–79
    Pecan Bars, 66–67
    Raspberry Streusel Bars, 68–69
    Strawberry Squares, 82–83
    Vanilla Pudding Bars, 64
Benefit Your Life, ix
Berries. see also Names of individual berries
    Berry Dessert Pancake, 180
    Fruit Jam, 221
    Summer Berry Bake, 179
    Summery Berry Gratin, 176
Berry Dessert Pancake, 180
Blackberries
    Fresh Fruit Cobbler with Soft Cookie
    Topping, 172–173
    Individual Blackberry-Walnut Buckles, 185
Blackberry-Walnut Buckles, 185
Blackstrap molasses, xii
    Gingerbread Cake, 93–94
    Gingerbread Cake with Dried Fruit, 94
    Molasses Spice Cookies, 23
    Molasses Spice Cookies with Dark Rum
    Glaze, 24–25
    Molasses Spice Cookies with Orange
    Essence, 27

Thick and Chewy Gingerbread
    Cookies, 51
Blondies, 75
Blueberries
    Blueberry Buckle, 182–183
    Fresh Blueberry Crumble, 168
    Summer Berry Bake, 179
Blueberry Buckle, 182–183
Blueberry Crumble, 168–169
Bourbon, in Pecan Bars, 66–67
Bread Pudding, 208
Brownies
    Fudgy, 60
    Lunchbox, 59
Bundt Cake, Glazed Chocolate, 112–113

Cacao/cacao nibs
    Almond Blossom Cookies, 32–33
    Almond Fudge Bars, 76–77
    as topping for Paleo Marshmallows, 88
    Blondies, 75
    Chewy Chocolate Cookies, 35
    Chocolate Almond Meal Cookies with Dried
    Cranberries, 12–13
    Chocolate Chip Cookies, 36
    Chocolate Cream Pie, 126–127
    Chocolate Cupcakes, 107
    Chocolate Icebox Cookies, 44
    Chocolate Mousse, 195
    Chocolate Nibs, 195
    Chocolate Pudding, 199
    Chocolate Sheet Cake, 110–111
    Chocolate Truffle Tart, 155
    Chocolate-Banana Pudding, 200
    Chocolate-Walnut Tart, 156–159
    decorating glazes using, 53
    Espresso Truffle Tart, 160
    Fudgy Brownies, 60
    German Chocolate Cake, 114–115
    Lunchbox Brownies, 59
    Warm Chocolate Fudge Cakes, 117
Cakes
    Almond Meal Cake With Broiled Icing, 100–101
    Applesauce Snack Cake, 90–91
    Carrot Cake, 122
    Chocolate Sheet Cake, 110–111
    German Chocolate Cake, 114–115
    Gingerbread Cake, 93
    Gingerbread Cake with Dried Fruit, 94
    Glazed Chocolate Bundt Cake, 112–113

Individual Bananas Foster Cakes, 104–105
Italian Almond Cake, 103
Lazy Daisy Cake, 98–99
Lemon Pound Cake, 121
Pineapple Cake, 118
Warm Chocolate Fudge Cake, 117
Cane syrup, xii
Canned coconut milk, x
Carrot Cake, 122
Chewy Chocolate Cookies, 35
Chilled Lemon Mousse with Raspberry Sauce, 196
Chocolate Almond Meal Cookies with Dried
    Cranberries, 12–13
Chocolate Chip Cookies, 36
Chocolate Cream Pie, 126–127
Chocolate Cupcakes, 107
Chocolate Frosting, 215
Chocolate frosting, 111
Chocolate Frosting with Orange Essence, 216
Chocolate Fudge Cakes, 117
Chocolate Icebox Cookies, 44
Chocolate Milkshake, 191
Chocolate Mousse, 195
Chocolate Pudding, 199
Chocolate Sheet Cake, 110–111
Chocolate Truffle Tart, 155
Chocolate-Banana Pudding, 200
Chocolate-Walnut Tart, 156–159
Cider-Baked Apples with Dried Cranberries, 186
Classic Tart Dough, 135
Cobbler, Fresh Fruit, 172–173
Coconut
    Almond Meal Cake With Broiled
    Icing, 100–101
    Coconut Frosting, 218
    Lazy Daisy Cake, 98–99
    Pecan Coconut Frosting, 219
Coconut flour, ix
Coconut Frosting, 218
Coconut oil, ix
Conversions with equivalencies, 223–225
Cookies
    Almond Blossom Cookies, 32–33
    Almond Butter Cookies, 39
    Almond Prune Cookies, 4
    Almond Raisin Cookies, 3
    Chewy Chocolate Cookies, 35
    Chocolate Almond Meal Cookies with Dried
    Cranberries, 12
    Chocolate Chip Cookies, 36

Chocolate Icebox Cookies, 44
Ginger-Almond Cookies, 7
Gingered Sugar Cookies, 16
Holiday Cookies, 52–53
Jam Sandwiches, 55
Jam Thumbprints, 30–31
Lebkuchen, 28–29
Lemon Sugar Cookies, 20
Lime Sugar Cookies, 19
Molasses Spice Cookies, 23
Molasses Spice Cookies with Dark Rum
Glaze, 24–25
Molasses Spice Cookies with Orange
Essence, 27
Nutty Almond Cookies, 11
Orange Almond Cookies, 8
Pine Nut-Raisin Icebox Cookies, 47
Sugar Cookies, 15
Thick and Chewy Gingerbread
Cookies, 51
Vanilla Icebox, 43
Cranberries
Chocolate Almond Meal Cookies with Dried
Cranberries, 12–13
Cider-Baked Apples with Dried Cranberries, 186
Cranberry-Pecan Tart, 146–147
Gingerbread Cake with Dried Fruit, 94
Cranberry-Pecan Tart, 146–147
Crème Brûlée, 108
Crisps
Apple Crisp, 165
Fresh Peach Crisp, 170–171
Crumble, Fresh Blueberry, 168–169
Cupcakes, Chocolate, 107

Dark chocolate, xii
Dates, in chocolate chip cookies, 36
Dried fruit, gingerbread cake with, 94

Eggs, x–xi
Espresso Truffle Tart, 160
Espresso/espresso powder
Almond Fudge Bars, 76–77
Chocolate Cupcakes, 107
Chocolate Sheet Cake, 110–111
Espresso Truffle Tart, 160
Glazed Chocolate Bundt Cake, 112–113
Mocha Frappe, 192

Fahrenheit to Celsius conversions, 224–225
Fahrenheit to Gas Mark (Imperial) conversions,
224–225
Fig Bars, 84–85
Frappe, mocha, 192
Fresh Blueberry Crumble, 168–169
Fresh Fruit Cobbler with Soft Cookie Topping, 172–173
Fresh Peach Crisp, 170–171
Frostings. see also Glazes
Chocolate, 215
Chocolate Cupcake, 107
Chocolate Frosting with Orange Essence, 216
Chocolate Sheet Cake, 110, 111
Coconut Frosting, 218
German Chocolate Cake, 114
Pecan Coconut Frosting, 219
Fruit. see individual types of fruits
Fruit Jam, 221
Apricot Squares, 80–81
decorating glazes, 53
Italian Almond Cake, 103
Jam Sandwiches, 55
Peach Squares, 78–79
Poached Apple Tart, 138–139
Raspberry Streusel Bars, 68–69
Strawberry Squares, 82–83
Fudgy Brownies, 60

German Chocolate Cake, 114–115
Ginger-Almond Cookies, 7
Gingerbread Cake, 93
Gingerbread Cake with Dried Fruit, 94
Gingerbread Cookies, 51
Gingered Sugar Cookies, 16
Glazed Chocolate Bundt Cake, 112–113
Glazes. see also Frostings
Dark Rum, 24, 25
Holiday Cookie, 53
Lebkuchen, 28, 29
Lemon Pound Cake, 121
Poached Apple Tart, 138
Poached Pear and Almond Tart, 140
vanilla, 112, 113

Hazelnuts
Lebkuchen, 28–29
Linzertorte, 149–151
Holiday cookie dough, for Jam
Sandwiches, 55

Holiday Cookies, 52–53
Honey, xi
Honeyville, ix

Icebox cookies
    Chocolate, 44
    Pine Nut-Raisin Icebox Cookies, 47
    Vanilla, 43
Icing, Broiled, 98. see also Frostings
Individual Bananas Foster Cakes, 104–105
Individual Blackberry-Walnut Buckles, 185
Italian Almond Cake, 103

Jam Sandwiches, 55
Jam Thumbprints, 30–31
JK Gourmet, ix

Key Lime Bars, 72
Key Lime Pie, 129

Lazy Daisy Cake, 98–99
Lebkuchen, 28–29
Lemon Pound Cake, 121
Lemon Squares, 71
Lemon Sugar Cookies, 20
Lemon Tart, 152–153
Lime
    Key Lime Bars, 72
    Key Lime Pie, 129
Lime Sugar cookies, 19–20
Lime Sugar Cookies, 19–20
Linzertorte, 149–151
Lunchbox Brownies, 59

Maple syrup, xi–xii
Marshmallows. See Paleo Marshmallows
Metric, volume conversions
    to, 223–224
Milkshakes, chocolate, 191
Mocha Frappe, 192
Molasses, xii
Molasses Spice Cookies, 23
Molasses Spice Cookies with Dark
    Rum Glaze, 24–25
Molasses Spice Cookies with Orange
    Essence, 27
Mousse
    chilled lemon, 196
    chocolate, 195

Nuts. see also Names of individual nuts
    Pine Nut-Raisin Icebox Cookies, 47
    Prune-Nut Bread, 97
Nutty Almond Cookies, 11

Orange Almond Cookies, 8
Orange Essence
    Chocolate Frosting with, 216
    Molasses Spice Cookies, 27
Oven temperature conversions, 224–225

Paleo jam. See Fruit Jam
Paleo Marshmallows
    Almond Butter Pie, 130
    Almond Fudge Bars, 76–77
    recipe, 87–88
Palm sugar, x
Pancake, berry dessert, 180
Pantry, items to stock in, ix–xii
Peach Crisp, 170–171
Peach Squares, 78–79
Peach-Vanilla Pudding, 207
Peaches
    Fresh Peach Crisp, 170–171
    Peach Squares, 78–79
    Peach-Vanilla Pudding, 207
Pears, Poached Pear and Almond Tart, 140–143
Pecan Bars, 66–67
Pecan Coconut Frosting, 219
Pecan Sandies, 48
Pecans
    Chocolate Almond Meal Cookies with
        Dried Cranberries, 12–13
    Cranberry-Pecan Tart, 146–147
    Pecan Bars, 66–67
    Pecan Coconut Frosting, 219
    Pecan Sandies, 48
    Raspberry Streusel Bars, 68–69
Pies
    Almond Butter Pie, 130
    Chocolate Cream Pie, 126–127
    Key Lime Pie, 129
    whoopie, 63
Pine Nut-Raisin Icebox Cookies, 47
Pineapple Cake, 118
Poached Apple Tart, 138–139
Poached apples, 138
Poached Pear and Almond Tart, 140–143
Prune-Nut Bread, 97

Prunes
    Almond Prune Cookies, 4
    Chocolate Chip Cookies, 36
Puddings
    Bread Pudding, 208
    Chocolate, 199
    Chocolate-Banana, 200
    Peach-Vanilla, 207
    Rich and Creamy Banana Pudding, 211
    Strawberry-Vanilla Pudding, 204
    Vanilla, 203

Raisins
    Almond Raisin Cookies, 3
    Gingerbread Cake with Dried Fruit, 94
    Pine Nut-Raisin Icebox Cookies, 47
Raspberries/ raspberry jam
    Bakes Raspberry Tart, 144–145
    Chilled Lemon Mousse with Raspberry Sauce, 196
    Jam Thumbprints, 30–31
    Linzertorte, 149–151
    Raspberry Streusel Bars, 68–69
    Summer Berry Bake, 179
Raspberry sauce, 196
Raspberry Streusel Bars, 68–69
Raw honey, xi
Rich and Creamy Banana Pudding, 211
Rum
    Individual Bananas Foster Cakes, 104–105
    Molasses Spice Cookies with Dark Rum
    Glaze, 24–25
    Pecan Bars, 66–67

Second molasses, xii
Skillet Apple Brown Betty, 175
Snack Cake, Applesauce, 90–91
Soft cookie topping, fruit cobbler
    with, 172–173
Spice Cookies, Molasses, 23
Strawberries
    Strawberry Squares, 82–83
    Strawberry Tart, 136–137
    Strawberry-Vanilla Pudding, 204
    Vanilla Pudding Bars, 64
Strawberry Shortcakes, 166
Strawberry Squares, 82–83
Strawberry Tart, 136–137
Strawberry-Vanilla Pudding, 204
Streusel
    Apricot Squares, 80–81

Blueberry Buckle, 182–183
Peach Squares, 78–79
Raspberry Streusel Bars, 68–69
Strawberry Squares, 82–83
Sugar Cookies, 15
    Gingered Sugar Cookies, 16
    Lemon Sugar Cookies, 20
    Lime Sugar Cookies, 19
Summer Berry Bake, 179
Summer Berry Gratin, 176

Tapioca flour, xi
Tapioca pearls, xi
Tart Dough, Classic, 135
Tarts
    Baked Raspberry Tart, 144–145
    Chocolate Truffle Tart, 155
    Chocolate-Walnut Tart, 156–159
    Cranberry-Pecan Tart, 146–147
    Espresso Truffle Tart, 160
    Lemon Tart, 152–153
    Linzertorte, 149–151
    Poached Apple Tart, 138–139
    Poached Pear and Almond Tart, 140–143
    Strawberry Tart, 136–137

Vanilla extract, xii
Vanilla glaze, 112, 113
Vanilla Icebox Cookies, 43
Vanilla Pudding, 203
    Whoopie Pies, 63
Vanilla Pudding Bars, 64
Virgin coconut oil (VCO), ix
Volume conversions U.S. to metric, 223–224

Walnuts
    Chocolate-Walnut Tart, 156–159
    Individual Blackberry-Walnut Buckles, 185
    Lunchbox Brownies, 59
    Nutty Almond Cookies, 11
    Prune-Nut Bread, 97
Warm Chocolate Fudge Cakes, 117
White chocolate/white chocolate chips
    Blondies, 75
    Chocolate Mousse, 195
    Crème Brûlée, 108
    Whoopie Pies, 63
Whoopie Pies, 63